POETRY ALI

POETRY ALIVE
An anthology

SELECTED AND EDITED BY

E. L. BLACK

Formerly Principal of Middleton St George
College of Education

MACMILLAN

First published in 1984

10 9 8 7 6 5 4 3
00 99 98 97 96 95 94 93 92 91

Published by
MACMILLAN EDUCATION LTD
Houndmills, Basingstoke, Hampshire RG21 2XS
and London
Companies and representatives
throughout the world

Printed in the People's Republic of China

British Library Cataloguing in Publication Data
Black, E.L.
Poetry Alive
1. English Poetry, 20th century
I. Title
821'.914'08 PR1225
ISBN 0-333--35817-1

CONTENTS

PREFACE

This sequel to *Nine Modern Poets* draws on the rich resources of poetry being written by poets who are alive today. Any selection must of course be an individual one, and the reader should know the principles which lie behind the editor's choice.

Firstly, to make the volume truly representative of contemporary poetry, the poets are all still writing in 1984. Secondly, by including an American poet, Anne Stevenson, two Scottish poets, Edwin Morgan and Douglas Dunn, an Irish poet, Seamus Heaney, and a West Indian poet, Edward Brathwaite, the breadth of cultural sources which contribute to the body of poetry being written in the English language is emphasised. Thirdly, the editor has deliberately omitted the obscure: not only to make the book accessible to students in schools and colleges, but also to follow the general reaction against T. S. Eliot's comment in 1921 that poets must be 'difficult'; poets are now more likely to communicate their ideas and emotions to a wide audience than to limit their address to small cliques of enlightened friends.

The editor has also looked for poets who are candid realists and who are representative of the mainstream of contemporary poetry. Two of them, Philip Larkin and Ted Hughes, were in *Nine Modern Poets*; they have been included again here simply because no contemporary anthology could stand without them, but the poems of theirs that have been chosen are all new. Finally, the editor has aimed for breadth of subject matter; many of the poets in this book write about urban life as it really is, with its 'Acres of clinker, slag-heaps, roads', over which 'the evening sky disgorges chemicals in silence'. But other poets, notably Seamus Heaney and Ted Hughes, write with sincere admiration about the people who work on farms and the vitality of the animals and birds.

The recent history of English poetry, which has led us to this point, has been a vitally changing one. Early in this century, in about 1907, the Irish writer J. M. Synge put forward the view that 'Before verse can be human again, it must learn to be brutal'. This in fact came to happen with the Great War, when poets found that if they were to bring home to their readers the real and terrible nature of the modern trench warfare that they had experienced, they would have to achieve as complete a revolution in poetic technique as scientists were already achieving in the art of war.

In the 1930s, W. H. Auden and the other poets of his group expressed in their verse contemporary ideas about politics and psychology. During World War II Dylan Thomas achieved a personal kind of lyrical poetry that seemed very different from all that had preceded it. Then, in the 1950s, the poets who have been referred to as 'The Movement' urged that poetry needed to return to the traditional objectives of clarity, logical syntax and form. From time to time an enthusiastic anthologist has picked out for emphasis just *one* of these determinants in twentieth century poetry: for instance, in 1956 Robert Conquest published the anthology called *New Lines* with the object of showing that 'a genuine and healthy poetry of the new period has established itself', because the poets of his day believed that 'Poetry is written by and for the whole man, intellect, emotion, senses and all'. With similar confidence the editors of the 1982 Penguin anthology of *Contemporary British Poetry* enthusiastically announced that 'After a spell of lethargy, British poetry is once more undergoing a transition; a body of work has been created which demands, for its appreciation, a reformation of poetic taste'.

If we are to pick out the constant impulses behind contemporary poetry, they would probably include: the belief that every kind of experience is eligible for description, with no restrictions to a special literary language: the search for ever more versatile metres and forms to represent the rhythms of contemporary speech; and the inventive skill in choosing similes and metaphors from every aspect of modern life, so that a ship can be *scissoring* the sea, friendly Australians talking like *tin-openers*, and the surface of the Pacific Ocean reflecting like *sheets of plate-glass*.

But poetry is not simply the sum of accurate observation, honest recording, and the use of plain words. It may arise out of the language of the poet's contemporaries, but if it is crafted to become poetry rather than prose, then the language will be heightened and intensified; the imagery will be coloured and vitalised; the meaning will be concentrated and distilled. If the poetry presented here succeeds in its object, it will convey to us such experiences as we have either shared or can imagine ourselves sharing in the future, but in words more exact and compelling than we as amateurs would ever have found.

ACKNOWLEDGEMENTS

The editor and publishers wish to thank the following who have kindly given permission for the use of copyright material:

Carcanet New Press Limited for poems by Edwin Morgan, 'An Addition to the Family', 'The Old Man and the Sea', 'The Unspoken', 'Strawberries', 'Linoleum Chocolate', 'Trio', 'Glasgow Sonnet', 'Good Friday', 'Aberdeen Train', 'Che' from *Poems of Thirty Years.*

Faber & Faber Ltd for poems by Douglas Dunn, 'The Clothes Pit', 'Men of Terry Street', 'Ships' and 'A Removal from Terry Street' from *Terry Street*; 'The New Girls', 'Under the Stone' and 'Guerrillas' from *The Happier Life*; 'The Competition', 'Boys with Coats', 'White Fields' and 'The House Next Door' from *Love or Nothing*; and 'Washing the Coins' from *St Kilda's Parliament.* Poems by Seamus Heaney, 'Trout', 'Churning Day', 'Digging', 'Storm on the Island', 'The Diviner', 'Valediction' and 'Honeymoon Flight' from *Death of a Naturalist*; 'The Wife's Tale', 'Thatcher' and 'Requiem for the Croppies' from *Door into the Dark*; 'Rookery' and 'Getting On On the Railways'. Poems by Ted Hughes, 'Hawk Roosting', 'The Retired Colonel' and 'Pike' from *Lupercal*; 'Thistles' from *Wodwo*; 'Crow Hears Fate Knock on the Door' and 'Dawn's Rose' from *Crow*; 'Snow and Snow' and 'The Warm and the Cold' from *Season Songs*; 'The Horses' and 'Six Young Men' from *The Hawk in the Rain,* and 'Mill Ruins' from *Remains of Elmet.* Poems by Philip Larkin, 'To the Sea', 'Show Saturday', 'Going, Going', 'Homage to a Government' and 'The Explosion' from *High Windows*; 'Here', 'MCMXIV', 'Reference Back' and 'Self's the Man' from *The Whitsun Weddings.*

David Higham Associates, Ltd on behalf of Norman Nicholson for the poems 'Have you Been to London?', 'Boo to a Goose', 'The Black Guillemot', 'Cleator Moor', 'Egremont', 'On the Closing of Millom Ironworks: September 1968', 'To the River Duddon', 'On Duddon Marsh', 'St Luke's Summer', 'To the Memory of a Millom Musician', 'Old Man at a Cricket

Match', 'Bond Street', 'Whitehaven', 'Innocents' Day' from *Collected Poems.* On behalf of Elizabeth Jennings for the poems 'The Young Ones', 'My Grandmother', 'The Diamond Cutter', 'Old Woman', 'A Disabled Countryman', 'Mirrors', 'Skies', 'A Game of Cards', 'San Paolo Fuori Le Mura, Rome', 'Song for the Swifts' from *Collected Poems.* On behalf of Charles Causley for the poems 'HMS Glory at Sydney', 'Chief Petty Officer', 'Yelverton', 'Ballad of the Faithless Wife', 'Death of an Aircraft', 'Ballad for Katherine of Aragon', 'At the Grave of John Clare', 'Cowboy Song' and 'Timothy Winters' from *Collected Poems.*

The Marvell Press for the poem 'No Road' from *The Less Deceived* by Philip Larkin.

Oxford University Press for poems by Anne Stevenson, 'The Crush' from *Travelling Behind Glass: Selected Poems 1963–1973*, © 1974; 'The Sun Appears in November', 'North Sea Off Carnoustie', 'With my Sons at Boarhills', 'Mallaig Harbour Resembles Heaven in Spring' and 'Sunlight' from *Enough of Green*, © 1977; 'Poem to my Daughter', 'If I Could Paint Essences', 'Green Mountain, Black Mountain' (Parts I to IV), 'The Garden' and 'Swifts' from *Minute by Glass Minute* © 1982. Poems by Edward Kamau Brathwaite, 'The Emigrants', 'Leopard', 'South', 'Ogun', 'Littoral', 'Twine', 'Islands' and 'The New Ships'.

Vernon Scannell for his poems 'Picnic on the Lawn', 'Autumn', 'Here and Human', 'A Mystery at Euston', 'Schoolroom on a Wet Afternoon', 'A Kind of Hero', 'August 1914', 'The Great War', 'Gunpowder Plot' and 'End of a Season'.

The University of Georgia Press for poems by Tony Connor, 'The Poet's District', 'October in Clowes Park', 'The Burglary', 'My Mother's Husband' and 'Lodgers' from *New and Selected Poems*, and 'Old Men', 'Druid's Circle' and 'Above Penmaenmawr'.

ACKNOWLEDGEMENTS

The authors and publishers wish to acknowledge the following photograph sources:

British Tourist Authority, p. 160 Faber & Faber, p. 60 Fay Godwin's Photo Files, pp. 94, 126 David Higham Associates Ltd/Photo: Parkers, London, p. 26 Jessie Anne Matthew, p. 142 Oxford University Press, pp. xvi, 200 Ann Pasternak Slater, p. 78.

The publishers have made every effort to trace the copyright holders but where they have failed to do so they will be pleased to make the necessary arrangements at the first opportunity.

EDWARD BRATHWAITE

Although Edward Kamau Brathwaite has spent most of his adult life as a member of the History faculty of the University of the West Indies in Jamaica, his native island was the Caribbean island of Barbados. He was born there in 1930 and, as he later wrote, 'sound of the sea came in at my window'. Barbados is in the extreme south-east of the West Indian islands; as a poet he found that its social set-up and geological structure were a great stimulus to his writing, and he realised how much of his own character was due to the impact of his native landscape upon him. Moreover, as a historian he became very much aware of how the benign characteristics of Barbados, an English-speaking island, had shaped his character. He was fascinated by the various effects that living in Barbados had had on the mentality of its Negro inhabitants over the centuries. In some ways the people, bullied and thrashed by their overseers during the centuries of slavery, lost their independence and courage; in more subtle and various ways the porous limestone and lethargic streams of Barbados left the Negroes 'indentured to the merchant's law' and to 'the merchant's whip'.

The many violent changes of scene and location that the Negroes endured when they were shipped from Africa to the West Indies as slaves helped rob them of their power and nerve. Yet in many ways they defiantly and resolutely behaved as though they were still in Africa.

After receiving a secondary education in Barbados, Brathwaite went to Pembroke College, Cambridge to read history, and then obtained a post in Ghana, which had just won its independence. While studying he became interested in aspects of the history of the coloured races that are often neglected by English students. For instance, he tried to find out how the spread of diseases such as syphilis had led to the decline of the Amerindian populations who lived in the West Indies before Columbus arrived. That is why Brathwaite, remembering all the different factors that reduced the native population, asks the question about Columbus:

'did his vision
fashion, as he watched the shore,
the slaughter that his soldiers
furthered here?'

Brathwaite also studied the attempts of the Negroes, dispossessed of their African homelands and shipped to the New World as slaves, to create a distinctive culture of their own. He was resolved to trace all the population movements, inside and outside Africa, that had had so much influence on the development of the Negroes. The Negro empires that had flourished in Sudan and West Africa just after 1100 had soon declined, and there were many movements of population inside Africa before the descendants of these West African tribes moved to the coast further south where they were rounded up by the European and Arab slave-traders and shipped to the New World. The continual and repeated migrations inside Africa during what Europeans call the Middle Ages helped to make the Negroes rootless. Brathwaite eventually made this subject the main topic of his poems *Rights of Passage* (1967), *Islands* (1969) and *Masks* (1981). In these poems he creates a counterpoint between the southward movements of his ancestors towards the slaving ports of tropical Africa and his own journey of exploration as he set out to reach the villages from which they began their migration. He deliberately mixes past and present: as he moves northwards from the coast to the inland village of his origins, his ancestors move down through the equatorial forests to meet him. In order to investigate the legacy of the past he makes repeated use of flashbacks and switches in time. Frequently he describes the past in the present tense in order to highlight the immediacy of past events. So he seems to travel back to the past in the company of his migrating ancestors. Some of this past was remote and glorious; for instance, he reminds his readers:

'we kept
our state on golden stools – remember?'

But he moves his reader from medieval Timbuctu to Takoradi, which was not built until the 1920s. He makes an unusual amalgam of the many different African and West Indian factors that influenced the history of the Negro slaves and their later descendants.

At one stage in his academic life Brathwaite wrote a thesis for the University of Sussex on the Development of Creole Society in Jamaica. The creole language was a mixture of French and English; it had been created by the mixed races that survive in the West Indies today. As a poet, Brathwaite makes new and creative uses of Creole vocabulary, and also of West Indian rhythms, incorporating in his poetry those that are typical of West Indian music.

If we analyse the linguistic methods by which he achieves this, we find that he uses unusual forms of pronouns, such as using *e* for *him*; that he uses unusual forms of verbs, especially auxiliary verbs, such as transposing passive and active or singular and plural, or past and present; and that he uses, more often than Standard English does, the type of transference where 'the yard of the warehouse' becomes 'the warehouse yard'. Moreover, Brathwaite changes the whole structure of some sentences; for instance, he writes:

> 'and the island resolving from water
>
> steep steps of blue
> and the anchor clumping the bottom,
> tapping of water along sides of the ship
>
> lapping away into silence;
> breath on my face
> where the palm trees were . . .'

In order to make sense of this we have to infer some phrase before *breath* such as 'all these blow a salt. . . .'

Various African influences began to affect the rhythm and metre of Brathwaite's poetry. He imitated and re-used the rhythms of African drumming and of those forms of Caribbean music that derive from Africa. He began to make an individual use of elision, which leaves the sound of a word suspended and so produces a hypnotic rhythmic tension.

He made original uses of internal rhyme as in the following lines:

'Watch now these hard men, *cold*
clear *eye'd* like the water we *ride*,
skilful with sail and the rope and the tackle

Watch now these *cold* men, *bold*
as the water banging the bow in a sudden wild *tide* . . .'

His distinctive uses of rhyme are also illustrated by the next extract:

'*Down down*
white
man, con
man, *brown*
man, *frown-*
ing fat
man that
lives in
the *town*.'

As well as the repetition of words that rhyme with *down*, there is the deliberately half-hidden weak rhyme between *fat* and *that*.

Brathwaite, like most West Indian poets, had begun to write poetry as an imitator of English verse forms. But English poetry is dominated by the alternate stresses of the iambic pentameter. For instance, Shakespeare's typical rhythm is that of:

'O, what a rogue and peasant slave am I!'

In the same way Gray begins his Elegy:

'The curfew tolls the knell of parting day.'

Even recently, a poet describing motor-cyclists used iambic pentameters with only a few variations on the regular metre:

'On motorcycles, up the road, they come:
Small, black, as flies hanging in heat, the Boys,
Until the distance throws them forth, their hum
Bulges to thunder held by calf and thigh.'

Brathwaite, unlike his fellow West Indian poet, Derek Walcott, felt that it was unnatural for West Indians to write in iambic pentameters, and was sure that he must get away from the iambic rhythm if his lines were to be vitalised by the feel of the Atlantic as it broke among the West Indian islands, by the beat of West Indian music, and by his intention to write in the new language of a new nation. Moreover, to undervalue this new language by calling it a mere dialect was to misunderstand its importance to West Indians.

Consequently, his poetry is intended to be read aloud rather than silently. If we hear it being read by a good West Indian speaker, we hear the rhythms that it is intended to recapture. Brathwaite thinks of the dance as an art form in which the African reaffirms his unity with the earth and sky, so to him it is essential that the reader of his poetry will bring into it the rhythms and cadences of African music and of the derived West Indian music that recreates the African vigour even after the long centuries of exile. Brathwaite is not trying to imitate in poetry what is better conveyed in music; he is trying to bring out the musical potential of words when they are used in the rhythmical combinations that are suggested by the Negroes' own musical forms. He believes that one of the great triumphs of the West Indians was to preserve the African dance in their American exile, and that it is essential for West Indian poetry to include what have been the most vital elements in African and West Indian dance.

The Emigrants

I

So you have seen them
with their cardboard grips,
felt hats, rain-
cloaks, the women
with their plain
or purple-tinted
coats hiding their fatten-
ed hips.

These are The Emigrants.
On sea-port quays
at airports
anywhere where there is ship
or train, swift
motor car, or jet
to travel faster than the breeze
you see them gathered:
passports stamped
their travel papers wrapped
in old disused news-
papers: lining their patient queues.

Where to?
They do not know.
Canada, the Panama
Canal, the Miss-
issippi painfields, Florida?
Or on to dock
at hissing smoke locked
Glasgow?

Why do they go?
They do not know.
Seeking a job
they settle for the very best
the agent has to offer:
jabbing a neighbour
out of work for four bob
less a week.

What do they hope for
What find there
these New World mariners
Columbus coursing kaffirs

What Cathay shores
for them are gleaming golden
what magic keys they carry to unlock
what gold endragoned doors?

2

Columbus from his after-
deck watched stars, absorbed in water,
melt in liquid amber drifting

through my summer air.
Now with morning, shadows lifting,
beaches stretched before him cold and clear.

Birds circled flapping flag and mizzen
mast: birds harshly hawking, without fear.
Discovery he sailed for was so near.

Columbus from his after-
deck watched heights he hoped for,
rocks he dreamed, rise solid from my simple water.

Parrots screamed. Soon he would touch
our land, his charted mind's desire.
The blue sky blessed the morning with its fire.

But did his vision
fashion, as he watched the shore,
the slaughter that his soldiers

furthered here? Pike
point and musket butt,
hot splintered courage, bones

cracked with bullet shot,
tipped black boot in my belly, the
whip's uncurled desire?

Columbus from his after-
deck saw bearded fig trees, yellow pouis
blazed like pollen and thin

waterfalls suspended in the green
as his eyes climbed towards the highest ridges
where our farms were hidden.

Now he was sure
he heard soft voices mocking in the leaves.
What did this journey mean, this

new world mean: dis-
covery? Or a return to terrors
he had sailed from, known before?

I watched him pause.

Then he was splashing silence.
Crabs snapped their claws
and scattered as he walked towards our shore.

EDWARD BRATHWAITE

Leopard

1
Caught therefore in this careful cage of glint, rock,

water ringing the islands'
doubt, his

terror dares
not blink. A nervous tick-

like itch picks
at the corners of his

lips. The lean flanks quick
and quiver until the

tension cracks his
ribs. If he could only

strike or trigger
off his fury. But cunning

cold bars break his
rage, and stretched to strike

his stretched claws strike
no glory.

2
There was a land not long
ago where it was other-
wise; where he was happy.

That fatal plunge down from the
tree on antelope or duiker,
was freedom for him then.

But somewhere in the dampened
dark the marks-
man watched, the strings were

stretched, the tricky traps were
ready. Yet had he felt
his supple force would fall

to such confinement,
would he, to dodge his doom
and guarantee his movement,

have paused from stalking deer
or striking down the duiker;
or would he, face to fate,

have merely murdered more?

3
But he must do
what fate had forced him to;

at birth his blood
was bent upon a flood

that forged him forward
on its deadly springs;

his paws grew heavy
and his claws shone sharp;

unleashed, his passion
slashed and mangled with its stainless

steel; no flesh he raped
would ever heal. Like grape

crushed in the mouth to you,
was each new death to him;

each death he dealt perfected him.
His victims felt this single

soft intention in him, as gentle
as a pigeon winging home.

4
Now he stands caged.
The monkeys lisp and leer
and rip and hammer
at their barriers;

he burns and paces;
turns again and paces,
disdaining admiration in those faces
that peer and pander at him

through the barriers.
Give him a tree to leap from,
liberator; in pity let him
once more move with his soft

spotted and untroubled splendour
among the thrills and whispers
of his glinting kingdom;
or unlock him and now let him

from his triggered branch
and guillotining vantage,
in one fine final falling
fall upon the quick fear-

footed deer or peer-
less antelope whose beauty,
ravaged with his sharp brutality,
propitiates the ancient guilt

each feels towards the other:
the victim's wish to hurt,
the hunter's not to;
and by this sacrifice

of strong to helpless other,
healed and aneled;
both hurt and hunter
by this fatal lunge made whole.

South

But today I recapture the islands'
bright beaches: blue mist from the ocean
rolling into the fishermen's houses.
By these shores I was born: sound of the sea
came in at my window, life heaved and breathed in me then
with the strength of that turbulent soil.

Since then I have travelled: moved far from the beaches:
sojourned in stoniest cities, walking the lands of the north
in sharp slanting sleet and the hail,
crossed countless saltless savannas and come
to this house in the forest where the shadows oppress me
and the only water is rain and the tepid taste of the river.

We who are born of the ocean can never seek solace
in rivers: their flowing runs on like our longing,
reproves us our lack of endeavour and purpose,
proves that our striving will founder on that.
We resent them this wisdom, this freedom: passing us
toiling, waiting and watching their cunning declension down to
the sea.

But today I would join you, travelling river,
borne down the years of your patientest flowing,
past pains that would wreck us, sorrows arrest us,
hatred that washes us up on the flats;
and moving on through the plains that receive us,
processioned in tumult, come to the sea.

Bright waves splash up from the rocks to refresh us,
blue sea-shells shift in their wake
and *there* is the thatch of the fishermen's houses, the path
made of pebbles, and look!
small urchins combing the beaches
look up from their traps to salute us:

they remember us just as we left them.
The fisherman, hawking the surf on this side
of the reef, stands up in his boat
and halloos us: a starfish lies in its pool.
And gulls, white sails slanted seaward,
fly into the limitless morning before us.

Ogun

My uncle made chairs, tables, balanced doors on, dug out
coffins, smoothing the white wood out

with plane and quick sandpaper until
it shone like his short-sighted glasses.

The knuckles of his hand were sil-
vered knobs of nails hit, hurt and flat-

tened out with blast of heavy hammer. He was
knock-knee'd, flat-
footed and his clip clop sandals slapped across the concrete

flooring of his little shop where canefield mulemen and a fleet
of Bedford lorry drivers dropped in to scratch
themselves and talk.

There was no shock of wood, no beam
of light mahogany his saw teeth couldn't handle

When shaping squares for locks, a key hole
care tapped rat tat tat upon the handle

of his humpbacked chisel. Cold
world of wood caught fire as he whittled: rectangle

window frames, the intersecting x of fold-
ing chairs, triangle

trellises, the donkey
box-cart in its squeaking square.

But he was poor and most days he was hungry.
Imported cabinets with mirrors, formica table

tops, spine-curving chairs made up of tubes, with hollow
steel-like bird bones that sat on rubber ploughs,

thin beds, stretched not on boards, but blue
  high-tensioned cables,
were what the world preferred.

And yet he had a block of wood that would have baffled them.
With knife and gimlet care he worked away at this on Sundays,

explored its knotted hurts, cutting his way
along its yellow whorls until his hands could feel

how it had swelled and shivered, breathing air,
its weathered green burning to rings of time,

its contoured grain still tuned to roots and water.
And as he cut, he heard the creak of forests:

green lizard faces gulped, grey memories with moth
eyes watched him from their shadows, soft

liquid tendrils leaked among the flowers
and a black rigid thunder he had never heard within his hammer

came stomping with the trunks. And as he worked
   within his shattered
Sunday shop, the wood took shape: dry shuttered

eyes, slack anciently everted lips, flat
ruined face, eaten by pox, ravaged by rat

and woodworm, dry cistern mouth, cracked
gullet crying for the desert, the heavy black

enduring jaw; lost pain, lost iron;
emerging woodwork image of his anger.

Littoral

I

In the bleached
stare of the one-
eye'd beach,
the fisherman
sits, his head
sleeps in the surf's
drone, his crossed
legs at home
on the rough sand.

His fingers work
shuttle and twine,
soft clack between
breakers and the whine
of the fine spume
flying off rock,
lapping his slack
nets, embroideries,
traps for the brine.

He is blind
so it is dark on the marked
shore for him now;
the sun's deep noon
steps back, steps
black, where the day-
light's footprint passes;
his eyes stare out like an empty shell,
its sockets of voices, wind,
grit, bits of conch, pebble;
his fingers knit as the dark rejoices
but he has his voices . . .

2
She's dark and her voice sings
of the dark river. Her eyes
hold the soft fire that only the warm
night knows. Her skin is musky and soft.

She travels far back, explores
ruins, touches on old immemorial legends
everyone but himself has forgotten. She
becomes warrior and queen and keeper of the tribe.

There is no fear
where she walks, although drums speak
to announce the immanent death of a tyrant;
and although her song is sad, there is no sorrow

where she sings; she walks in a world
where the river whispers of certainties
that only he can acknowledge. The trees

touch confident and unassuming. He hopes
that light will break in the clearing before her song ends . . .

3
But no light breaks under the decks
where the sails sing
and the island resolving from water

steep steps of blue
and the anchor clumping the bottom,
tapping of water along sides of the ship

lapping away into silence;
breath on my face
where the palm trees were,

blue drifting above them, birds
too high for shadow,
scuffed sand at my feet,

stone, roots of grass,
crushing scuttled sea shells,
claws of crabs

the soil shallow.
And I, Quaker,
praying,

my broad hat under the turmoil
of stars
and I, slaver,

slaying,
my bright whip ripping a new soil
of scars

buying
a new world of negroes, soil-
ing the stars.

4
So my island drifts
plundered by butterflies.
The dog lifts his mourning to heaven.

Who will till this soil
cutting straight fervours into the rock
whose marrow, whose toil

butting into this sweat-sweetened rot
will soften these roots,
loosen the shoots under pebble and shale?

How will the dry fruit warm
at my fingers, the leaves'
spiders spin green winning webs,

shadows, lean working tissues
for moisture, for light
tricking the raindrop, trapping the blight?

EDWARD BRATHWAITE

Twine

My husband
if you cud see he
fragile, fraid o' e own shadow
he does let de man boss e 'bout in de job
like e got a dog in de corner

i know when i did first meet e
he did strong
smellin strong o carbolic lotion
an de dirty jokes he did tell de taffeta women on de excursion
train out to t'ickets

i know when i did first meet e
he did look like e cudda wrench de wrongs
off de sweet drink bottles wid e teef
an tek what he want *so*, an drink it

an he did wear dem two-tone shoes
an a wesscoat, an dat tie-pin, man,
you cud *wink* it

but if you look pun e now
fragile, 'fraid o' e own shadow
but he tired, man, but he tired

he never get none o dem free trip to europe
dat i hear de civil service servants talk 'bout
he never get no pension from de people

when de dust in dat warehouse yard brek up e lung,
get on bad in e chess, cough wrackle e up like a steel
donkey, most kill e, you hear, before he did passin good forty

he never know what name pension nor compensation
for all dem mornings dat i hads was to get up 'fore six
to mek tea, slice bread, an scrape an butter de crackle
an place it before e, so he cud get down to town before open

they int give e no prize nor no piece o paper
for all de years dat e stannin' up there countin canefields;
buckley, vaucluse, mount all, fairfield, bissix, clifton hall, small
. . .

de lorries slowly shippin up up de hill
de cane green, de cane ripe, de cane cut, de fields hot
cutlass sweet, cutlass sweat, cutlass singin

trash, windmill, crack, bubble o vat in de fac'try
load pun me head, load in de cart, de mill spinnin spinnin
spinnin
syrup, liquor, blood o de fields, flood o' the ages

my ghost in your footstep, my eyes red in the hunger of your
eyes
the lorries slowly shippin up up the hill
to the mill, to the fortress of bags in the warehouse, to the eyes

of my father

the merchant's clerk, the merchant's man, the merchant's
property
black to his poor backra money
back to his poor backra psalm.

Islands

So looking through a map
of the islands, you see
rocks, history's hot
lies, rot-
ting hulls, cannon
wheels, the sun's
slums: if you hate
us. Jewels,
if there is delight
in your eyes.

The light
shimmers on water,
the cunning
coral keeps it
blue.

Looking through a map
of the Antilles, you see how time
has trapped
its humble servants here. Descendants of the slave do not
lie in the lap
of the more fortunate
gods. The rat
in the warehouse is as much king
as the sugar he plunders.
But if your eyes
are kinder, you will observe
butterflies
how they fly higher
and higher before their hopė dries
with endeavour
and they fall among flies.

Looking through a map
of the islands, you see
that history teaches
that when hope
splinters, when the pieces
of broken glass lie
in the sunlight,
when only lust rules
the night, when the dust
is not swept out
of the houses,
when men make noises
louder than the sea's
voices; then the rope
will never unravel
its knots, the branding

iron's travelling flame that teaches
us pain, will never be
extinguished. The islands' jewels:
Saba, Barbuda, dry flat-
tened Antigua, will remain rocks,
dots, in the sky-blue frame
of the map.

The New Ships

I

Takoradi was hot.
Green struggled through red
as we landed.

Laterite lanes drifted off
into dust
into silence.

Mammies crowded with cloths,
flowered and laughed;
white teeth
smooth voices like pebbles
moved by the sea of their language.

Akwaaba they smiled
meaning welcome

akwaaba they called
aye kooo

well have you walked
have you journeyed

welcome.

You who have come
back a stranger
after three hundred years

welcome.

Here is a stool for
you; sit; do
you remember?

Here is water
dip
wash your hands
are you ready
to eat?

Here is plantain
here palm oil;
red, staining the fingers;
good for the heat,
for the sweat.

Do
you remember?

2
I tossed my net
but the net caught
no fish

I dipped a wish
but the well
was dry

Beware
beware
beware

I travelled to a distant town
I could not find my mother
I could not find my father
I could not hear the drum

Whose ancestor am I?

I walked in the bush
but my cut-
lass cut
no path;
returned
from the farm

but could not hear
my children laugh.

Beware
beware
beware

For now the long hot flintlocks sing with heat;
fever of quick sales
rot the branches

of bone; blood brands the bird's
full sails and trinkets
sear my flesh. Whose
brother, now, am I?

Could these soft huts
have held me?
wattle daubed on wall,
straw-hatted roofs,

seen my round or-
dering, when kicked to life
I cried
to the harsh light around me?

If you should see someone
coming this way
send help, send help, send help
for I am up to my eyes in fear.

CHARLES CAUSLEY

Charles Causley was born in Launceston, Cornwall, in 1917. He served in the Royal Navy from 1940 to 1946, then in 1947 he went to Peterborough to train as a teacher. It is noticeable that the subject-matter of most of his poems derives from his experiences in the Navy and from living in the south-western counties; but he has also written a group of poems that draw their subject-matter from the Peterborough area. After college, he taught for some years in Cornwall, but he has also held many part-time and temporary posts: he has been a member of the Arts Council, and a Visiting Fellow in Poetry at various universities. He received the Queen's Medal for Poetry in 1967 and has compiled a number of anthologies, such as *Peninsula: An Anthology of Verse from the West Country* (Macdonald, 1957), and the *Puffin Book of Magic Verse* (1974). His *Collected Poems 1951–1975* was published by Macmillan in 1975 and his verse play, *The Ballad of Aucassin and Nicolette*, was published by Kestrel Books in 1981.

Causley has excelled at writing ballads: straightforward narratives in short rhymed stanzas. Their naval breeziness conceals the skill and care with which they have been constructed. They seem fresh, spontaneous and genuine. The striking qualities of these poems are that they are easily understood and appeal at once to a wide audience; these obvious virtues make them very different from a lot of modern poetry, which often becomes obscure through trying to pack too much meaning into too few words. Yet Causley's language is undeniably modern and avoids all literary conventions. He has the ability to call a spade a spade in a jaunty, humorous way. He achieves a direct and realistic tone by using candid similes, such as when the narrator of *Yelverton* says that his wife's voice is like a *loud-hailer*, and by his use of naval metaphors, such as the clock in Helpston churchyard firing off the hour; similarly he says that the sudden bursts of inspired poetry in John Clare's verse are 'bursting like a diamond bomb'. He achieves a more complicated effect with his equally well perceived description of the hospital visitor:

> 'Ceaselessly firing all-purpose smiles
> At everyone present.
> She destroys hope
> In the breasts of the sick
> Who realize instantly
> That they are incapable of surmounting
> Her ferocious goodwill.'

Another example is his description of *HMS Glory* entering Sydney Harbour, in which he includes just those convincing homely details of the view that would strike the crew of the aircraft-carrier, and he makes us realise how boyishly thrilled the crew were to be 'stepping ashore in a new country' with clean shirts on and their pockets full of pound notes to spend in the bars, shops, theatres and cinemas of Sydney. In these and other ways he describes naval life during World War II as it really was. He draws slightly comic sketches of the grim non-commissioned officers who were so unimpressed when young sailors returned to barracks in Plymouth after becoming sun-tanned in Malta or the Pacific. But Causley never forgets that the Navy's losses during the war were tragically high, and death is a recurrent theme in his poetry:

> 'O war is a casual mistress
> And the world is her double bed.
> She has a few charms in her mechanised arms
> But you wake up and find yourself dead.'

The paradox of the last line is typical of the grim, laconic humour which Causley introduces into his most serious poetry.

In general terms Causley has some of the virtues, but also some of the limitations, that one associates with the poetry of Rudyard Kipling. Like Kipling, Causley makes clever occasional use of anapaest metre and internal rhymes in lines like 'The way of the lynx and the angry Sphinx' or – to repeat the line quoted above – 'She has a few charms in her mechanised arms'. Most of all, Causley reminds us of the comment by T. S. Eliot on Kipling's poetry that 'We expect to have to defend a poet against the charge of obscurity; we have to defend Kipling against the charge of excessive lucidity'. Both poets have the qualities of a good journalist, and both write a wider variety of types of poetry than is immediately apparent. Indeed we might appropriately apply some sentences to Kipling and Causley that T. S. Eliot originally applied to Kipling and Dryden:

> 'Both were masters of phrase, both employed rather simple rhythms with adroit variations; and by both the medium was employed to convey a simple forceful statement rather than a musical pattern of emotional overtones . . . They arrived at poetry through eloquence; for both, wisdom has the primacy over inspiration; and both are more concerned with the world about them than with their own joys and sorrows.'

CHARLES CAUSLEY

'HMS Glory' at Sydney

August 1945

Now it seems an old forgotten fable:
The snow goose descending on the still lagoon,
The trees of summer flowering ice and fire
And the sun coming up on the Blue Mountains.

But I remember, I remember Sydney,
Our bows scissoring the green cloth of the sea,
Prefaced by plunging dolphins we approached her:
The land of the kookaburra and the eucalyptus tree.

The harbour bridge, suddenly sketched by Whistler,
Appeared gently on a horizon of smudges and pearls,
And the sun came up behind us
With a banging of drums from the Solomons.

O! I shall never forget you on that crystal morning!
Your immense harbour, your smother of deep green trees.
The skyscrapers, waterfront shacks, parks and radio-towers,
And the tiny pilot-boat, the *Captain Cook*,
Steaming to meet us:
Our gallery deck fringed with the pale curious faces of sailors
Off the morning watch.

O like maidens preparing for the court ball
We pressed our number-one suits,
Borrowing electric irons and starching prim white collars,
And stepped forth into the golden light
With Australian pound notes in our pockets.

O there is no music
Like the music of the Royal Marine bugler
Sounding off *Liberty men*.
And there is no thrill
Like stepping ashore in a new country
With a clean shirt and with pound notes in your pocket.

O Sydney, how can I celebrate you
Sitting here in Cornwall like an old maid
With a bookful of notes and old letters?

I remember the circular bar in Castlereagh Street
And the crowds of friendly Aussies with accents like tin
 openers,
Fighting for schooners of onion beer.
I remember Janie, magnificent, with red hair,
Dressed in black, with violets on her reliable bosom,
Remembering a hundred names and handling the beer engines
With the grace and skill of ten boxers.

O Janie, have the races at Melbourne seen you this year?
And do matelots, blushing, still bring you flowers?
Across three continents: across monsoon, desert, jungle, city,
Across flights of rare birds in burning Africa,
Across crowds of murderous pilgrims struggling grimly to
 Mecca,
Across silver assaults of flying-fish in the Arabian Sea,
I salute you and your city.

I remember the deep canyons of streets, the great shafts of
 sunlight
Striking on fruit-shop, flower-shop, tram and bookstall,
The disappearing cry of the Underground Railway,
The films: *Alexander Nevsky* and *Salome*,
The plays: *Macbeth* and *Noah* in North Sydney,
And travelling there, across the fantastic bridge,
Our ship, the *Glory*, a lighted beetle,
A brilliant sarcophagus far below
On the waterfront at Woolloomoolloo.

O yes, I remember Woolloomoolloo,
The slums with wrought-iron balconies
Upon which one expected to find, asleep in a deck-chair,
Asleep in the golden sun, fat, grotesque and belching:
Captain Cook.

The Chinese laundries, the yellow children in plum-coloured
  brocade,
The way they fried the eggs, the oysters and champagne.
I remember Daphne and Lily, the black-market gin,
And crawling back to the docks as the dawn
Cracked on my head.

O the museum with the gigantic, terrifying kangaroo,
Who lived, as huge as a fairy story,
Only ten thousand years ago.

O the sheepskin coats, the woollen ties,
And our wanderings in David Jones' store
Among a rubble of silk stockings and tins of fruit salad.
The books I bought at Angus & Robertson's bookshop,
Sir Osbert Sitwell, and Q (to remind me of home).

I remember the ships and ferries at Circular Quay,
And the tram ride to Botany Bay,
So magnificently like the postage stamp
I bought as a child.
I remember the enormous jail at La Perouse,
The warders on the walls with their rifles.
I remember the Zoo at Taronga Park,
The basking shark I gazed down at in terror,
And the shoes I wore out walking, walking.

And so I celebrate this southern city
To which I shall never return.
I celebrate her fondly, as an old lover,
And I celebrate the names and faces of my companions:

George Swayne, Ron Brunt, Joney,
Tug Wilson, Jan Love, Reg Gilmore,
Pony Moor, Derby Kelly, Mac,

Where are they now?

Now it seems an old forgotten fable:
The snow goose descending on the still lagoon,
The trees of summer flowering ice and fire
And the sun coming up on the Blue Mountains.

Chief Petty Officer

He is older than the naval side of British history,
And sits
More permanent than the spider in the enormous wall.
His barefoot, coal-burning soul
Expands, puffs like a toad, in the convict air
Of the Royal Naval Barracks at Devonport.

Here, in depot, is his stone Nirvana:
More real than the opium pipes,
The uninteresting relics of his Edwardian foreign commission.
And, from his thick stone box,
He surveys with a prehistoric eye the hostilities-only ratings.

He has the face of the dinosaur
That sometimes stares from old Victorian naval photographs:
That of some elderly lieutenant
With boots and a celluloid Crippen collar,
Brass buttons and cruel ambitious eyes of almond.

He was probably made a Freemason in Hong Kong.
He has a son (on War Work) in the Dockyard,
And an appalling daughter
In the WRNS.
He writes on your draft-chit,
Tobacco-permit or request-form
In a huge antique Borstal hand,
And pins notices on the board in the Chiefs' Mess
Requesting his messmates not to
Lay on the billiard table.
He is an anti-Semite, and has somewhat reactionary views,
And reads the pictures in the daily news.

And when you return from the nervous Pacific
Where the seas
Shift like sheets of plate glass in the dazzling morning;
Or when you return
Browner than Alexander, from Malta,
Where you have leaned over the side, in harbour,
And seen in the clear water
The salmon-tins, wrecks and tiny explosions of crystal fish,
A whole war later
He will still be sitting under a pusser's clock
Waiting for tot-time,
His narrow forehead ruffled by the Jutland wind.

Yelverton

I met her by the Rifle Range
  Among the spent cartridges and the heather.
Gay she was as a pin-table
  And a voice like a loud-hailer.

I was stationed in Devonport at the time
  Among the jolly stokers, the yellow-faced
Dark-haired sick-bay tiffies, the Mongolian Chief Yeomen.
  And, for quiet, I came out on a bus to the moor.

Here, by the church of battleship grey,
  The auctioneers' advertisements, the sound of water,
Among the lovely ponies and the fat golfers
  I met her by the Rifle Range.

And so, when peace came, I never returned to Glasgow.
  Now I work as a fitter in the dockyard
And, I might say, as an ex-service man
  I was lucky to get the job.

We've a nice little place here at Yelverton,
  And although it's a bit chilly in winter
There's plenty of room on the moor for the kiddies
  And we have nice little outings to Princetown.

All the same, I am sure you will see
  Why I do not wish to join the Rifle Club?
Myself, on the long winter evenings,
  I find myself thinking of the Royal Naval Barracks at
    Devonport:

Remembering the jolly stokers, the yellow-faced
  Dark-haired sick-bay tiffies, the Mongolian Chief Yeomen,
And, behind the backcloth of cranes and acetylene welders,
  The splendid sea.

Ballad of the Faithless Wife

Carry her down to the river
  Carry her down to the sea
Let the bully-boys stare at her braided hair
  But never a glance from me.

Down by the writhing water
  Down by the innocent sand
They laid my bride by the toiling tide
  A stone in her rifled hand.

Under the dainty eagle
  Under the ravening dove
Under a high and healthy sky
  I waited for my love.

Off she ran with a soldier
  Tall as a summer tree,
Soft as a mouse he came to my house
  And stole my love from me.

O splintered were all the windows
  And broken all the chairs
War like a knife ran through my life
  And the blood ran down the stairs.

Loud on the singing morning
  I hear the mad birds rise
Safe from harm to the sun's alarm
  As the sound of fighting dies.

I would hang my harp on the branches
  And weep all through the day
But stranger, see! The wounded tree
  Has burned itself away.

False O false was my lover
  Dead on the diamond shore
White as a fleece, for her name was Peace
  And the soldier's name was War.

CHARLES CAUSLEY

Death of an Aircraft

An incident of the Cretan campaign, 1941

One day on our village in the month of July
An aeroplane sank from the sea of the sky,
  White as a whale it smashed on the shore
  Bleeding oil and petrol all over the floor.

The Germans advanced in the vertical heat
To save the dead plane from the people of Crete,
  And round the glass wreck in a circus of snow
  Set seven mechanical sentries to go.

Seven stalking spiders about the sharp sun
Clicking like clockwork and each with a gun,
  But at 'Come to the cookhouse' they wheeled about
  And sat down to sausages and *sauerkraut*.

Down from the mountain burning so brown
Wriggled three heroes from Kastelo town,
  Deep in the sand they silently sank
  And each struck a match for a petrol tank.

Up went the plane in a feather of fire
As the bubbling boys began to retire
  And, grey in the guardhouse, seven Berliners
  Lost their stripes as well as their dinners.

Down in the village, at murder-stations,
The Germans fell in friends and relations:
  But not a Kastelian snapped an eye
  As he spat in the air and prepared to die.

Not a Kastelian whispered a word
Dressed with the dust to be massacred,
  And squinted up at the sky with a frown
  As three bubbly boys came walking down.

One was sent to the county gaol
Too young for bullets if not for bail,
  But the other two were in prime condition
  To take on a load of ammunition.

In Archontiki they stood in the weather
Naked, hungry, chained together:
  Stark as the stones in the market place,
  Under the eyes of the populace.

Their irons unlocked as their naked hearts
They faced the squad and their funeral-carts.
  The Captain cried, 'Before you're away
  Is there any last word you'd like to say?'

'I want no words,' said one, 'with my lead,
Only some water to cool my head.'
  'Water,' the other said, ' 's all very fine
  But I'll be taking a glass of wine.

A glass of wine for the afternoon
With permission to sing a signature tune!'
  And he ran the *raki* down his throat
  And took a deep breath for the leading note.

But before the squad could shoot or say
Like the impala he leapt away
  Over the rifles, under the biers,
  The bullets rattling round his ears.

'Run!' they cried to the boy of stone
Who now stood there in the street alone,
  But, 'Rather than bring revenge on your head
  It is better for me to die,' he said.

The soldiers turned their machine-guns round
And shot him down with a dreadful sound
  Scrubbed his face with perpetual dark
  And rubbed it out like a pencil mark.

But his comrade slept in the olive tree
And sailed by night on the gnawing sea,
   The soldier's silver shilling earned
   And, armed like an archangel, returned.

A Ballad for Katharine of Aragon

Queen of England, 1509–1533
Buried in Peterborough Cathedral

As I walked down by the river
Down by the frozen fen
I saw the grey cathedral
With the eyes of a child of ten.
O the railway arch is smoky
As the Flying Scot goes by
And but for the Education Act
Go Jumper Cross and I.

But war is a bitter bugle
That all must learn to blow
And it didn't take long to stop the song
In the dirty Italian snow.
O war is a casual mistress
And the world is her double bed.
She has a few charms in her mechanised arms
But you wake up and find yourself dead.

The olive tree in winter
Casts her banner down
And the priest in white and scarlet
Comes up from the muddy town.
O never more will Jumper
Watch the Flying Scot go by.
His funeral knell was a six-inch shell
Singing across the sky.

The Queen of Castile has a daughter
Who won't come home again.
She lies in the grey cathedral
Under the arms of Spain.
O the Queen of Castile has a daughter
Torn out by the roots,
Her lovely breast in a cold stone chest
Under the farmers' boots.

Now I like a Spanish party
And many O many's the day
I have watched them swim as the night came dim
In Algeciras Bay.
O the high sierra was thunder
And the seven-branched river of Spain
Came down to the sea to plunder
The heart of the sailor again.

O shall I leap in the river
And knock upon paradise door
For a gunner of twenty-seven and a half
And a queen of twenty-four?
From the almond tree by the river
I watch the sky with a groan,
For Jumper and Kate are always out late
And I lie here alone.

CHARLES CAUSLEY

At the Grave of John Clare

Walking in the scythed churchyard, around the locked church,
Walking among the oaks and snails and mossed inscriptions
At first we failed to find the grave
But a girl said 'There he is: there is John Clare.'
And we stood, silent, by the ridged stone,
A stone of grey cheese.
There were no flowers for the dead ploughman
As the gilt clock fired off the hour,
Only the words:
A poet is born not made.

The dove-grey village lay in the Dutch landscape:
The level-crossing and the fields of wet barley,
The almshouses, the school, the Ebenezer Chapel,
The two pubs, and the signposts
To Stamford, To Maxey
From the pages of biography.
And later, sitting in the church
Among the unstuffed hassocks,
And smoking a pipe on the gate
At Maxey Crossing,
I thought of the dead poet:

Of the books and letters in the Peterborough Museum,
The huge, mad writing.
Of the way he walked, with one foot in the furrow,
Or hurried, terrified, as a child to fetch the flour from Maxey
Expecting from every turn a Caliban.
Of London, Charles Lamb and Hazlitt,
The bad grammar, the spelling, the invented words,
And the poetry bursting like a diamond bomb.
I thought of the last days, the old man
Sitting alone in the porch of All Saints' in Northampton,
And the dead poet trundling home to Helpston.

O Clare! Your poetry clear, translucent
As your lovely name,
I salute you with tears.
And, coming out on the green from the Parting Pot,
I notice a bicycle tyre
Hanging from the high stone feathers of your monument.

Cowboy Song

I come from Salem County
  Where the silver melons grow,
Where the wheat is sweet as an angel's feet
  And the zithering zephyrs blow.
I walk the blue bone-orchard
  In the apple-blossom snow,
When the teasy bees take their honeyed ease
  And the marmalade moon hangs low.

My Maw sleeps prone on the prairie
  In a boulder eiderdown,
Where the pickled stars in their little jam-jars
  Hang in a hoop to town.
I haven't seen Paw since a Sunday
  In eighteen seventy-three
When he packed his snap in a bitty mess-trap
  And said he'd be home by tea.

Fled is my fancy sister
  All weeping like the willow,
And dead is the brother I loved like no other
  Who once did share my pillow.
I fly the florid water
  Where run the seven geese round,
O the townsfolk talk to see me walk
  Six inches off the ground.

Across the map of midnight
  I trawl the turning sky,
In my green glass the salt fleets pass
  The moon her fire-float by.
The girls go gay in the valley
  When the boys come down from the farm,
Don't run, my joy, from a poor cowboy,
  I won't do you no harm.

The bread of my twentieth birthday
  I buttered with the sun,
Though I sharpen my eyes with lovers' lies
  I'll never see twenty-one.
Light is my shirt with lilies,
  And lined with lead my hood,
On my face as I pass is a plate of brass,
  And my suit is made of wood.

CHARLES CAUSLEY

Timothy Winters

Timothy Winters comes to school
With eyes as wide as a football pool,
Ears like bombs and teeth like splinters:
A blitz of a boy is Timothy Winters.

His belly is white, his neck is dark,
And his hair is an exclamation mark.
His clothes are enough to scare a crow
And through his britches the blue winds blow.

When teacher talks he won't hear a word
And he shoots down dead the arithmetic-bird,
He licks the patterns off his plate
And he's not even heard of the Welfare State.

Timothy Winters has bloody feet
And he lives in a house on Suez Street,
He sleeps in a sack on the kitchen floor
And they say there aren't boys like him any more.

Old Man Winters likes his beer
And his missus ran off with a bombardier,
Grandma sits in the grate with a gin
And Timothy's dosed with an aspirin.

The Welfare Worker lies awake
But the law's as tricky as a ten-foot snake,
So Timothy Winters drinks his cup
And slowly goes on growing up.

At Morning Prayers the Master helves
For children less fortunate than ourselves,
And the loudest response in the room is when
Timothy Winters roars 'Amen!'

So come one angel, come on ten:
Timothy Winters says 'Amen
Amen amen amen amen.'
Timothy Winters, Lord.
   Amen.

TONY CONNOR

Tony Connor is an interesting modern example of a person who has achieved success as a writer, and even as an academic critic of poetry, without having had a conventional education. He was born in a working-class district of Manchester in 1930. As he explains in his poetry, his father soon deserted his mother, and he left school at the age of fourteen. From 1948 to 1950 he served as a tank driver in the Royal Inniskilling Dragoon Guards. On being demobilised he obtained a job in Manchester as a textile designer, but during this time he began to write poetry. In 1961 he became an Assistant Lecturer in Liberal Studies at Bolton Technical College. He was encouraged to continue writing poetry by the personal praise of the principal, A. J. Jenkinson, who had written a realistic book called *What do Boys and Girls Read?* (This book pleads that more *modern* literature should be read in schools.) He was also encouraged by the success of *A Taste of Honey*, Shelagh Delaney's play about working-class life in Salford, the town that adjoined Manchester until local boundaries were changed in the 1970s and it became part of Greater Manchester.

Tony Connor is one of the few poets who have given an honest, up-to-date account of the industrial towns of Britain – especially of those in the north of England. He has put into poetry the attitude and the voice of the people who live in these northern working-class areas, so it is a little surprising that his poetry has won a higher reputation in the United States than in this country. American critics have praised him as 'one of the poets bringing new and authentic life to English poetry'. Because of the respect that his poetry has won in the USA he has been appointed to a series of lectureships – and finally professorships – at American universities.

The variety of style and topics that he achieves as a poet should not be underestimated, yet it is true that most of his best and sharpest poems deal candidly with his experience of Manchester and Salford as a boy. They look at the world in the way that the working class of northern England have traditionally looked at it. For instance, in some of his poems he writes with enthusiasm and candour about the games that he and other young boys played in urban streets after dark. As we read *The Poet's District*, for example, Connor makes us feel that we are playing tag with him on winter nights, running from gas-lamp to gas-lamp, then taking short cuts through the neglected gardens at the back of the bigger houses in an area that is steadily going down the social scale and becoming more unfashionable. He describes straightforwardly a scruffy park which fails to achieve genuine beauty, especially on misty autumn afternoons, but which provides opportunities for courting couples to find their 'true kingdom' in it, in defiance of their drab surroundings and which provides opportunities for hardy boys to shake down the last sour fruit of the pear trees, and to go fishing – with or without a licence.

Connor draws an authentic picture of the northern side of Manchester and Salford, and he is honest and brilliantly vivid as he includes its less romantic aspects. For instance, he mentions that the October sunlight in Clowes Park is grudgingly reflected by the glazed bricks of the ladies' lavatory, and he is amused by the closeness of a modern fish-and-chip shop to the pompous nineteenth-century tombs in the churchyard of St Mark's, Cheetham Hill. Such details are true of any industrial town, but Connor is unusually successful and sincere in including them in his poetry. Consequently the impressions that he gives of the appearance and life of towns are unassuming and undistorted.

As well as being a vivid observer of what Manchester and Salford looked like between 1940 and 1970, Connor is also a shrewd judge of the gritty northern character. He understands the attitude of his prim, disappointed mother to her unreliable husband, who deserted her. He understands the complex attitudes of lonely landladies to their rather disappointing single lodgers. He understands, and presents sympathetically, the disadvantages of choosing burglary as a trade.

Although most of his poems keep to a limited range of topics, this does not produce any feeling of sameness. He writes in an unacademic, independent style, making us share his intense interest in the everyday events and emotions of working-class life. Although he uses rhyme successfully and naturally in a minority of his poems, his most typical ones are unrhymed, and grasp our attention by their hard-biting directness. He writes as though he has never been influenced by anyone else's poetry and seems to model himself on no one, yet he must have been stimulated and encouraged by other modern poets who have written realistically and straightforwardly about modern scenes and people. Victoria Sackville-West summed up the craftsmanship of such writers by saying that:

> 'All things designed to play a faithful part
> Build up their plain particular poetry.'

But though Connor's poems are *plain* in the sense of being clear and outspoken, they are not *plain* in the sense of being dull. He demonstrates true craftsmanship in the way he uses sharp, personal phrases to combine a truthful and witty style. He highlights the surprises and contrasts of town life. His style is capable of achieving a considerable variety of effects. For instance, he can produce a fine, poetical, resonant line when his subject demands this, or he can produce the vinegary tartness and irony with which he accuses society of neglecting the old men who had done in their time all that society demanded of them, yet lived on to be *flattered* by overconfident comedians and *studied* by condescending sociologists.

For all these reasons we welcome the unusual clarity with which Tony Connor has drawn scenes and characters from urban life, and the candid, confident style in which he holds our attention.

TONY CONNOR

The Poet's District

My mind runs on, and back, and round;
routes of my childhood fixed the shape
of thought; I cannot now escape
shadowy entries, streets that wind,
alleys that are often blind.

The games I played on winter nights –
chancing a labyrinth of dark
limbos between the gaslamps – mark
me one who races fears and doubts
with bated breath, whose short cuts

are tumbling trespasses through sad
gardens abandoned by the rich,
whose hints to pursuers, roughly scratched
arrows on brick and cryptic words
only with difficulty deciphered.

Bounded by solitude, and walls,
and brews that peter out on crofts,
concealed corners, sudden shifts
of level, backs that flirt with ginnels –
double round privies – skirt schools,

deviously beneath the close
horizons of houses, through streets
grown nightmare-still, I take thought
towards that final hiding place
where someone crouches with my face

waiting impatient to be found
and freed by a swift, relieving tig.
I am small and fearful. Very big
and quiet, and cold, and unconcerned,
the tricky district of my mind.

October in Clowes Park

The day dispossessed of light. At four o'clock
in the afternoon, a sulphurous, manufactured
twilight, smudging the scummed lake's far side,
leant on the park. Sounds, muffled –
as if the lolling muck clogged them at the source –
crawled to the ear. A skyed ball thudded
to ground, a swan leathered its wings by the island.
I stood and watched a water-hen arrow
shutting silver across the sooty mat
of the lake's surface, an earl's lake,
though these fifty years the corporation's,
and what is left of the extensive estate –
a few acres of scruffy, flat land
framing this wet sore in the minds of property agents –
a public park. All else is built on.
Through swags of trees poked the bare backsides
of encircling villas, garages, gardening-sheds,
a ring of lights making the park dimmer.
Boys and men shouldering long rods –
all licensed fishers, by their open way –
scuffled the cinders past me, heading for home,
but I stayed on; the dispossessed day
held me, turned me towards the ruined Hall.
Pulsing in that yellow, luminous, murk
(a trick of the eye), the bits of broken pillar
built into banks, the last upright wall,
the stalactite-hung split shells of stables,
seemed likely to find a voice – such pent-in grief
and anger! – or perhaps to explode silently
with force greater than any known to progress,
wiping the district, town, kingdom, age,
to darkness far deeper than that which fluffed
now at the neat new urinal's outline,
and heaved and beat behind it in the ruins.
Like a thud in the head, suddenly become memory,
stillness was dumb around me. Scrambling up
a heap of refuse, I grabbed at crystalled brick.

Flakes fell from my hand – a gruff tinkle –
no knowledge there of what brought the Hall low,
or concern either. Neither did I care.
Irrecoverably dead, slumped in rank weed
and billowy grass, it mouldered from here to now,
connoting nothing but where my anger stood
and grief enough to pull the sagging smoke down
from the sky, a silent, lethal, swaddling
over the garden I played in as a child,
and over those children – laughter in the branches –
shaking the pear-tree's last sour fruit to ground

The Burglary

It's two o'clock now; somebody's pausing in the street
to turn up his collar. The night's black: distraught
with chimney-toppling wind and harsh rain –
see, the wet's soaking in on the end-gable,
and the frothing torrent, overspilling the broken drain,

accosts the pavement with incoherent babble.
There is the house we want: how easy to burgle,
with its dark trees, and the lawn set back from the road;
the owners will be in bed now – the old couple;
you've got the position of the safe? – Yes, I know the code.

The cock's going mad up there on the church steeple;
the wind's enormous – will it ever stifle;
still, its noise, and the rains are with us, I daresay,
they'll cover what we make, if we go careful
round by the greenhouse, and in at the back way.

Here's the broken sash I mentioned; – no need to be fearful,
watch how I do it: these fingers are facile
with the practice I've had on worse nights than this.
I tell you, the whole thing's going to be a doddle:
the way I've got it worked out, we can't miss.

Although, God knows, most things turn out a muddle,
and it only confuses more to look for a moral.
Wherever I've been the wind and the rain's blown; –
I've done my best to hang on, as they tried to whittle
the name from the action, the flesh away from the bone,

but I think, sometimes, I'm fighting a losing battle.
So many bad nights; so many strange homes to burgle,
and every job done with a mate I don't know: –
oh, you're all right; I don't mean to be personal,
but when the day breaks, you'll have your orders, and go.

Then, the next time the foul weather howls in the ginnel;
when the slates slide, the brimming gutters gurgle;
there'll be another lad I've never seen before,
with the rest of the knowledge that makes the job possible
as I ease up a window or skeleton-key a door.

Still, it's my only life, and I've no quarrel
with the boss's methods; – apart from the odd quibble
about allowances and fair rates of pay,
or the difficult routes I often have to travel,
or the fact that I never get a holiday.

Most of the time, though, I'm glad of mere survival,
even at the stormiest hour of the darkest vigil
. . . Here's the hall door; under the stairs, you said?
This one's easy, because the old folk are feeble,
and lie in their curtained room, sleeping like the dead.

Sometimes, believe me, it's a lot more trouble,
when you've got to be silent, and move as though through
   treacle.
Now hold your breath while I let these tumblers click . . .
I've done these many a time . . . a well known model;
one more turn now . . . Yes; that does the trick.

Nothing inside? The same recurrent muddle;
I think the most careful plan's a bloody marvel
if it plays you true, if nothing at all goes wrong.

Well, let's be off; we've another place to tackle
under the blown, black rain; and the dawn won't be long

when the wind will drop, and the rain become a drizzle,
and you'll go your way. Leaving me the bedraggled
remnants of night, that walk within the head
long after the sun-shot gutters cease to trickle,
and I draw my curtains, and topple into bed.

Old Men

When there was war they went to war,
when there was peace they went to the labour exchange,
or carried hods on an hour's notice.
If their complaints were heard in Heaven
no earthly sign was given.

They have suffered obscurely a bleak recurring dream
many lifetimes long. Wounded and gassed
for noble causes they were not thought fit to understand
made idle to satisfy the greed of their betters
lectured when it suited the State
ignored when it suited the State
flattered by comedians
studied by young sociologists,
they have survived to be cosseted by the Regional Hospital
Board.

They sit on a low stone wall in front of The Home
in an afternoon sun that shines like new,
grateful to have been allowed so much.

They puff black pipes.
Their small eyes see dead wives and children who emigrated.
They talk about the evening meal
and that old bugger George who's going senile.

When they walk in they tread gingerly,
not trusting the earth to stay beneath them for much longer.

TONY CONNOR

My Mother's Husband

My mother worries more
as she grows old, about that period
when he was at home. Not that she ever
admits to doubt of her ramrod-
straight honesty's perfect right
to feel outraged at his behaviour,
not that she says there was some wrong
on her side too – no matter how little.
The way her mind turns back
is like a child retracing steps on a dark night,
vainly scrabbling ground for the bright
coin it had gone to purchase sweets with –
unable, even, to find the hole
through which it must have slipped.

Sometimes she makes a joke
of how her conscience settled
all the bills he let go hang
when he disappeared, or of her luck
in picking such a fool
of a man from all the ones she kept
dangling from her little finger.
More often, though, she sees his criminal streak
as author of her tragedy,
unfailingly lumping with it, even now
not daring to consider longer –
his cruel trick
of being different; deliberately
taking the other side, the opposite view
from 'everyone else'. I think of my
serious clashes with her rigid mind;
her closings, with a blind:
'You're getting like your father.'

At seventy, there are certain new
infinitesimal hints of tone-
changes in the iron mockery
with which she tells of how he'd go
miles to hear a thing called 'Lohengrin',
and how she's seen him, thick with lather –
foaming from ear to ear –
posturing at the mirror like a loon,
reciting soliloquies from Shakespeare.

Lodgers

They came with somewhere else in view,
but scrambled to retrieve my ball,
and smiled and told me tales. I grew
within their shadows: Chew, and Nall,
Entwistle, Mounsor, Mitcham, Grey –
masterful men who could not stay.

Some boozed and came in late, and some
kept to their bedrooms every night,
some liked a joke, and some were glum,
and all of them were always right.
Unwitting fathers; how their deep
voices come back to me in sleep!

I hear them mumbling through the wall
nursery prayers and drunken smut;
I see their hairy fingers maul
sandwiches delicately cut;
I smell their smoky suits, their sweat;
salute them all, and own my debt.

They came; they fidgeted; they went.
Able to settle nowhere long,
theirs were the terms of banishment
that clothe the skeleton. Their strong
fathering figures could afford
little beyond their bed and board.

And yet, enough. Each exile's mite
of manhood noble in its fall
bestowed upon me, helped me write
a name on nothing. Chew, and Nall,
Entwistle, Mounsor, Mitcham, Grey –
masterful men who could not stay.

Druid's Circle

The few squat leaning rocks in a loose ring
are a disappointment to all that climb
the mountain track to see them. They are nothing
like Auschwitz, Belsen, or Buchenwald. No crime

against humanity lingers in the air
of this place. The so-called 'Sacrificial
Stone' is a boring flat expanse, bare
of any hint of blood. It doesn't look especial

in the least – except for the roughly scratched
initials: a confused palimpsest
of clumsy letters cross-hatched
on its surface. To most people the trip's a waste

of time, and, if the women shudder,
the men light pipes, the children fret,
it is the wild-eyed ba-ba and scatter
of all that moving mutton, the sight

of so much horizon, and the air,
so appalling in its emptiness,
that makes them loath to explore further,
and sends them townwards, laughing with distress.

TONY CONNOR

Above Penmaenmawr

The upland farmers have all gone;
the lane they laid twists without purpose,
visiting broken gates and overgrown
gardens, to end in clumps of gorse.

Their unroofed houses, and fallen barns,
rich in nettles, lie dead in hiding
from the wind that howls off Talyfan's
saw-tooth ridge; their walls divide

bracken from bracken; their little church
of bare rock has outlasted use:
hikers' signatures in the porch,
'Keys obtainable at the Guesthouse.'

Yet, not to sentimentalize,
their faces turned from drudgery
when the chance showed itself. There is
hardly a sign of the husbandry

of even the last to leave – so slight
was their acceptance by the land.
They left for the seaside towns, to get
easier jobs, and cash in hand.

Five miles of uplands, and beyond –
a thousand feet below – the coast,
its bright lights twinkling, freezing wind
dragging the cloud down like a frost

from Talyfan. Alone upon
these darkening, silent heights, my fears
stay stubbornly with the farmers, gone
after six hundred thankless years.

DOUGLAS DUNN

Douglas Dunn is comparable to Connor in that he too has written authentic poetry about the working-class people of Britain's industrial towns. He was born in 1942 in Inchinnan, Renfrewshire, Scotland. He was educated at Renfrew High School; at Camphill School, Paisley; at the Scottish School of Librarianship; and at the University of Hull. From 1966 to 1971 he was employed by the University Library, where the University Librarian happened to be Dunn's fellow-poet, Philip Larkin. During the 1960s, 1970s and 1980s Dunn published several volumes of poetry, including *Terry Street*, *The Happier Life*, *Love or Nothing*, *Barbarians*, and *St Kilda's Parliament*.

Dunn's poetry concentrates on two main themes – his observations of the working-class people of Hull, and his memories from his boyhood days of the more respectable, Scottish working class. In developing the first theme he writes sympathetically about the lively, but not very successful, inhabitants of a neglected and unimpressive part of Hull. They live in the unprepossessing houses of an area which he calls Terry Street. He praises them in a tone which suggests that he is a lodger in one of the houses in the street who does not quite fit in. He is always looking out of the window – in admiration rather than curiosity – to see what his fascinating neighbours are up to. He gives the impression that he remains an outsider, envying the vitality and dare-devil attitudes of Terry Street's inhabitants, but he does not seem to join in the fun himself.

The young women of Terry Street catch his eye. They try desperately hard to be up-to-date in their appearance, and this compels them to work hard at their sewing-machines in order to make the new clothes that will keep them in the forefront of fashion. They have to make their clothes for themselves in order to make ends meet. They are so resolved to equip themselves with the newest type of shoe that they must spend a large proportion of their money on fancy footwear. The brightness of their clothes shows that they are idealists and optimists, dreaming of – and dressing for – a happy world where the sun shines more brilliantly than it does in Hull, and where boyfriends are better mannered than their slightly uncouth lovers.

The young men of Terry Street are less fashion-conscious than their womenfolk, and less sure of themselves, especially in their hours of leisure, which they do not quite know how to fill. But as soon as they grow a few years older they gain the self-confidence of eccentrics and begin to appear as characters. For instance, the ex-serviceman whose war wound has turned him into a cripple with an insurmountable limp, still walks fast and boyishly in a brave attempt to conquer and defy his disability. Similarly, the man whose brothers-in-law are helping him to perform a 'moonlight flit', and leave his rooms without paying his arrears of rent, is taking with him – of all improbable pieces of property – a lawnmower! Even the ne'er-do-wells who beg off the people queueing for the Saturday-night cinema, and who spend their daylight hours sleeping off their drinking, seem *splendid barbarians* in the eyes of Dunn.

Dunn's poems about his other main theme – his Scottish boyhood – are less simple, partly because he feels that he is an exile from both Scotland and his childhood. In these poems he switches to and fro between the past and the present, between the attitude that he felt as a lad to the events that he describes and the more complicated attitude of the adult Dunn who is writing a mature poem about the same events. For instance, Dunn the boy and Dunn the poet react differently to his mother's well-meaning attempt to comfort him by assuring him that photographs of wartime horrors, and other reminders of man's inhumanity to man, were only 'photographs in a terrible past'.

At the same time Dunn emphasises how many different classes – or at least subsections of classes – existed in the Scotland of the 1945 to 1970 period. Dunn's family belonged firmly to the upper working class. He envied the children of farmers who were brought to school in cars, and he enjoyed stealing apples from the farmers' orchards. He shouted rude words at the daughters of the farmers, whose ancestors he accused of disinheriting his own. Similarly he despised as privileged the boy from a private school who wore a brown school uniform when he sat in the bus in front of Dunn and called him 'a poor boy' – to Dunn's puzzled surprise, for both of them carried identical toy Hurricane fighter-planes. As a boy Dunn felt a sharp enough feeling of class hatred and social envy to force himself to run faster by pretending that his competitors were privileged members of a presumptuous upper class. On the other hand Dunn's parents were well enough off for him to feel sorry for the boy without a coat whom the prim conductress would not allow on the bus. Moreover, Dunn's parents could afford to take him from Scotland to London, to see in the Motor Show the actual staff car that Montgomery had used at the Battle of El Alamein.

One of Dunn's successes is to write poems which sound very much like working-class speech. They assume that the listener (or reader) is familiar with the subject and characters that he is talking about, which is an accurate observation of what working-class raconteurs often do. His characters never stop to explain the essential points, but leave listeners (or readers) to deduce for themselves such details as what sort of street Terry Street might be. These poems rarely rhyme, but they contain a vivid and varied vocabulary; and although they include some words or phrases (e.g. *intellectual grooming* or *inarticulate paradise*) that working-class people would not use, their fundamental honesty and directness gives the over-all impression that we are listening to working-class speech. Dunn achieves this effect through the naturalness and modernity of his vocabulary, but he is skilful enough to manage this without descending to the swear words that seem obligatory to some rather desperate contemporary poets in their frantic attempts to sound up-to-date and honest. Dunn has chosen his topics so appropriately and has shaped his material so professionally that he leaves us with an impression of his talent as well as his candour. Moreover he usually ends his poems – even his short ones – with an emphatic epigrammatic statement that says the last word on the subject very neatly, such as when he describes his disappointment that his gift of a toy aeroplane to a poorer boy had achieved so little, for:

> 'my lost Hurricane
> Solved nothing in the sleet and rain.'

Similarly he sums up the natural, undramatic behaviour of the men of Terry Street by saying that:

> 'They hold up their children and sing to
> them.'

In these ways Dunn's poetry combines a direct representation of modern working-class life with a gift for choosing assertive images and illustrations as well as colourful and eloquent phrases. His poems demonstrate the virtues of the very best photographs: they focus on a small, clearly defined subject and present it with clarity and emphasis. In addition, they keep surprising us by the brilliance of their phrase-making.

DOUGLAS DUNN

The Clothes Pit

The young women are obsessed with beauty.
Their old fashioned sewing machines rattle in Terry Street.
They must keep up, they must keep up.

They wear teasing skirts and latest shoes,
Lush, impermanent coats, American cosmetics.
But they lack intellectual grooming.

In the culture of clothes and little philosophies,
They only have clothes. They do not need to be seen
Carrying a copy of *International Times*,

Or the Liverpool Poets, the wish to justify their looks
With things beyond themselves. They mix up colours,
And somehow they are often fat and unlovely.

They don't get high on pot, but get sick on cheap
Spanish Burgundy, or beer in rampant pubs,
And come home supported and kissed and bad-tempered.

But they have clothes, bright enough to show they dream
Of places other than this, an inarticulate paradise,
Eating exotic fowl in sunshine with courteous boys.

Three girls go down the street with the summer wind.
The litter of pop rhetoric blows down Terry Street,
Bounces past their feet, into their lives.

Men of Terry Street

They come in at night, leave in the early morning.
I hear their footsteps, the ticking of bicycle chains,
Sudden blasts of motorcycles, whimpering of vans.
Somehow I am either in bed, or the curtains are drawn.

This masculine invisibility makes gods of them,
A pantheon of boots and overalls.
But when you see them, home early from work
Or at their Sunday leisure, they are too tired

And bored to look long at comfortably.
It hurts to see their faces, too sad or too jovial.
They quicken their step at the smell of cooking,
They hold up their children and sing to them.

A Removal from Terry Street

On a squeaking cart, they push the usual stuff,
A mattress, bed ends, cups, carpets, chairs,
Four paperback westerns. Two whistling youths
In surplus U.S. Army battle-jackets
Remove their sister's goods. Her husband
Follows, carrying on his shoulders the son
Whose mischief we are glad to see removed,
And pushing, of all things, a lawnmower.
There is no grass in Terry Street. The worms
Come up cracks in concrete yards in moonlight.
That man, I wish him well. I wish him grass.

DOUGLAS DUNN

The New Girls

The dancing and drinking go on into the night
In the rooms of Edwardian houses,
In flats that cads and fashionable young couples rent,
Where the parties of Saturday happen
After the pub everyone goes to has closed.

There are always the girls there no one's seen before,
Who soon become known and their first names remembered.
Replacing the girls who 'simply just vanished'
To new jobs in London or husbands who've quietened down.
The new girls leave with the men who brought them

To rooms nearby in the same district, or one just like it.
At dawn, three streets from their homes,
The girls leave cars with doors that slam,
Engines that sound like men's contemptuous laughter,
As they disappear at fifty down an empty street.

Then they reach the door, and turn the key, and know
They have been listening to their own footsteps
In the silence of Sunday before the milkmen,
When the cats are coming home to eat, and water dripping
From the bridge is heard a hundred yards away.

Under the Stone

They sleep out the day in Grimsby, Goole, or Hull,
The sleep of Empire sherry and unspeakable liquors,
And clumsily beg at the Saturday cinema queues
From steady workers and their penny-pinching girlfriends,
The washed and sober, who only want to laugh or listen.

These men remind them of the back of their minds.
Splendid barbarians, they form tribes in the slums
Up certain dim streets, the tribes of second-hand,
In empty houses no one wants to buy,
Abandoned rooms the poor have given up.

No one wants to see them, in a grey dawn, walk down
The empty streets, an army of unkept appointments,
Broken promises, as drab as fog,
Like portents meaning bad harvests, unemployment,
Cavalry in the streets, and children shouting 'Bread! Bread!'

But they mean nothing, they live under the stone.
They are their own failures and our nightmares
Or longings for squalor, the bad meanings we are.
They like it like that. It makes them happy,
Walking the rubble fields where once houses were.

Guerrillas

They lived on farms, were stout and freckled, knew
Our country differently, from work, not play.
Fathers or brothers brought them to school in cars,
Dung on the doors, fresh eggs in the back.
The teachers favoured them for their wealth,
Daffodils and free eggs, and we envied them
The ownership of all the land we roved on,
Their dangerous dogs and stately horses,
The fruit we had to steal, their land being
Income, and ours a mysterious provider.

They owned the shadows cast by every branch,
Chestnuts and flowers, water, the awkward wire.
Their sullen eyes demanded rent, and so
We shouted the bad words to their sisters,
Threw stones at hens, blocked up the froggy drains.
Outlaws from dark woods and quarries,
We plundered all we envied and had not got,
As if the disinherited from farther back
Came to our blood like a knife to a hand.

DOUGLAS DUNN

The Competition

When I was ten, going to Hamilton
On the Leyland bus named for Eddlewood,
A boy with an aeroplane just like mine
Zoomed at his war games in the seat in front.
I'd never seen such a school uniform –
As brown as the manure in Cousar's coup
Where someone's city cousin had jumped in
Having been told it was 'just sand' –
One of Glasgow's best fee-paying places,
Brown as barrowloads from the blue-bottled byre.
I couldn't help it; I had to talk to him
And tell him I, too, had a Hurricane.
His mother pulled him to her, he sat sullen,
As if I'd spoiled his game. I spoke again,
And he called me a poor boy, who should shut up.
I'd never thought of it like that.
The summer tenements were so dry I cried.
My grandfather wouldn't give *him* sixpence.

Years later, running in a race, barefooted
As I'd trained my spikes to ruin, convinced
My best competitor was him, I ran into
The worst weathers of pain, determined to win,
But on the last lap, inches from the tape, was beaten
By someone from Shotts Miners' Welfare Harriers Club.

Boys with Coats

When I was ten, outside the Govan Plaza,
My first day on the Glasgow Underground,
I gave a boy with no coat in the sleet and rain
My pocket-money and my model aeroplane.
He said he was going to Greenock, the place
For which our bus was named, 'via Inchinnan'
Where we lived in village comfort near
An aerodrome – *HMS Sanderling*,
Its concrete fields of war named for a bird
I'd never seen. 'My father's in Greenock,'
He said; but the conductress wouldn't let him on.
Faces through streaming windows stared contempt
To see him set off in the wet to Linthouse,
Where they all guessed he lived – the tenements
That frightened me because they were so dark.

I who had sat in Monty's staff car at the Motor Show,
Having been born on the night of Alamein
In the war that serving justice served injustice –
That boys with coats might give to those without,
Effacing rights of ownership with gifts –
Felt radical that my lost Hurricane
Solved nothing in the sleet and rain.

White Fields

An aeroplane, its red and green night-lights
Spotting its distant noise in the darkness;
'Jack Frost', you say, pointing to white fields
Sparkling. My eyes accept the dark, the fields
Extend, spreading and drifting, fences rising
Before the black hedge that zips beside the road
I'm told I must never try to cross without you.
'What time is it?' – 'The middle of the night!
You've had a dream, I heard you shout.'
It woke me and I cried aloud, until

My mother came and showed me the farm
Wasn't burning, the school still had its roof,
There was no one hidden in the little fir trees.
'Only an aeroplane!' As if you meant by that
That there in 1948 in Renfrewshire
We were safe from fear, and the white eyes
Of dead Jews were just photographs
In a terrible past, a neighbour's magazine.
'Only an aeroplane!' Unsleeping factories,
All night you busied overhead, and flames
Flushed out my cities made of shoe-boxes
And dominoes, my native village of shaws.
So innocent machine! I had a toy like you
That I made buzz and drone like Lelper's bees,
From which I dropped the A-bomb on John's pram,
Crumpling the hand-embroidered sheets.
  Our breath melted ice on the window-pane.
Fields drizzled on the glass, opening strips
Of short-lived clarity, and fingernails of ice
Slid to the sill. 'No harm will come to us.'
I slept. Till now I've slept, dreaming of mice
Burrowing under the crusted tufts of snow
That heaviest fall had left us with,
Our planet flooded into continents
Of stray, white islands, a sea too cold to swim.
Till now I've slept, and waking, I reject
Your generation, an old copy of *Everybody's*
Thrown out with *Film Fun* and the tea leaves,
Bulldozed by a conscript from our village
Into a pit dug by forced labour.
So easily is love shed, I hardly feel it.
  White fields, your angled frost filed sharply
Bright over undisturbed grasses, do not soothe
As similes of innocence or idle deaths
That must happen anyway, an unmoral blankness;
Be unforgiving stillness, natural, what is:
Crimes uttered in landscape, smoke-darkened snow.
  Trains in my distance altered. Cattle trucks
Seemed to chug through Georgetown, a station
Where a fat man in a black uniform kept hens

On the platform. The waggons sprouted arms
And dropped dung, and no one sang
'Ten Green Bottles' or 'The Sash'. Offensive outings.

Six years old! And I lived through the worst of it!

The House Next Door

Old dears gardening in fur coats
And 'Hush Puppies', though it's a mild July,
Once met Freddie Lonsdale at John o' Groats.
Their keyboard's Chopin and their humour's wry.
   There's no one I'd rather be called 'famous' by.
   They have an antique goldfish, a cat called Sly.

They live in my unpublished play
For two sad characters. Their Chippendale
Haunts England's salesrooms, their silver tray
That brought Victoria's breakfast and her mail.
   I visit their house – its coffee aroma,
   The cat out cold in its afternoon coma!

I watch them watching for the post,
Wondering who writes. In *my* play, no one writes,
They are alone, together, and have lost
Our century by being old. Their nights
   Are spent rehearsing through Irving Berlin;
   The gardens turn to stage-sets when they begin.

My best times with them are 'Chopin
Mornings'. They smile vainly at my small applause –
No one plays the Pole as badly as they can –
And Sly stands up, and purrs, stretching his claws,
   Playing his cat's piano on the cushions,
   And called by pianist sisters, Perfect Nuisance.

There garage is pronounced gar*age*,
Strawberries never known as strawbs, but *fraises*,
And cheddar is called cheese, the rest *fromage*,
And all life is a lonely Polonaise.
  Why do I love them, that milieu not mine,
  The youngest, laughingly, 'last of the line'?

No answers. They have given me
Too much for answering. I am their pet,
Like Sly. They have defied me, cutting free
From my invention. 'Let us live. Forget
  You made us up for money. We'll give you tea,
  And you shall drive our ancient crock down to the sea.'

Ships

When a ship passes at night on the Clyde,
Swans in the reeds picking oil from their feathers
Look up at the lights, the noise of new waves,
Against hill-climbing houses, malefic cranes.

A fine rain attaches itself to the ship like skin.
The lascars play poker, the Scottish mate looks
At the last lights, one that is Ayrshire,
Others on lonely rocks, or clubfooted peninsulas.

They leave restless boys without work in the river towns.
In their houses are fading pictures of fathers ringed
Among ships' complements in wartime, model destroyers,
Souvenirs from uncles deep in distant engine rooms.

Then the boys go out, down streets that look on water.
They say, "I could have gone with them,"
A thousand times to themselves in the glass cafés,
Over their American soft drinks, into their empty hands.

Washing the Coins

You'd start at seven, and then you'd bend your back
Until they let you stand up straight, your hands
Pressed on your kidneys as you groaned for lunch,
Thick sandwiches in grease-proofed bundles, piled
Beside the jackets by the hawthorn hedges.
And then you'd bend your little back again
Until they let you stand up straight. Your hands
On which the earth had dried in layers, itched, itched,
Though worse still was that ache along the tips
Of every picking finger, each broken nail
That scraped the ground for sprawled potatoes
The turning digger churned out of the drills.
Muttering strong Irish men and women worked
Quicker than local boys. You had to watch them.
They had the trick of sideways-bolted spuds
Fast to your ear, and the upset wire basket
That broke your heart but made the Irish laugh.
You moaned, complained, and learned the rules of work.
Your boots, enlarging as the day wore on,
Were weighted by the magnets of the earth,
And rain in the face was also to have
Something in common with bedraggled Irish.
You held your hands into the rain, then watched
Brown water drip along your chilling fingers
Until you saw the colour of your skin
Through rips disfiguring your gloves of mud.
It was the same for everyone. All day
That bead of sweat tickled your smeared nose
And a glance upwards would show you trees and clouds
In turbulent collusions of the sky
With ground and ground with sky, and you portrayed
Among the wretched of the native earth.
Towards the end you felt you understood
The happy rancour of the Irish howkers.
When dusk came down, you stood beside the byre
For the farmer's wife to pay the labour off.
And this is what I remember by the dark
Whitewash of the byre wall among shuffling boots.

She knew me, but she couldn't tell my face
From an Irish boy's, and she apologized
And roughed my hair as into my cupped hands
She poured a dozen pennies of the realm
And placed two florins there, then cupped her hands
Around my hands, like praying together.
It is not good to feel you have no future.
My clotted hands turned coins to muddy copper.
I tumbled all my coins upon our table.
My mother ran a basin of hot water.
We bathed my wages and we scrubbed them clean.
Once all that sediment was washed away,
That residue of field caked on my money,
I filled the basin to its brim with cold;
And when the water settled I could see
Two English kings among their drowned Britannias.

SEAMUS HEANEY

Seamus Heaney was born in 1939 in County Derry, which belongs to the rural north-west of Northern Ireland. Although many critics have argued that it is impossible for twentieth-century poets to convert the details of rural life into a convincing part of their subject-matter, Heaney, like the Welsh poet R. S. Thomas, is one of the minority who have succeeded in doing this. He has achieved in the twentieth century what Thomas Hardy achieved in the nineteenth: he has made the everyday facts of life on a farm seem a natural part of contemporary life.

Heaney was educated at St Columb's College, a Teachers' Training College in Londonderry, and later at Queen's University, Belfast. His early volumes of poetry such as *Death of a Naturalist* (1966), *Door into the Dark* (1969), *Wintering Out* (1973) and *North* (1975), won him an immediate reputation and literary acclaim (*North* won both the Duff Cooper Memorial Prize and the W. H. Smith Memorial Prize), and led to his being elected to various temporary lectureships in American and Irish universities.

His characteristic genius is shown in the skill with which he finds natural and simple, yet vivid, words to describe life and work on a farm. He enlivens his descriptions with brief glimpses of the curiosity and fright which he felt on occasions such as when a plague of frogs invaded a flax-dam, thus suggesting the title of his first volume, *Death of a Naturalist*. In this way he creates a fascinating and realistic picture of the old-fashioned moral way of life which existed in his boyhood.

As well as giving us clear pictures of agricultural operations and showing us how Irish farms looked in the 1940s, he draws convincing pen-portraits of the men and women who worked on the farms, and of the emotional relationships between them. The farms that he writes about were, if we stop to analyse them, slightly old-fashioned because little labour-saving machinery had been introduced. For instance, in *The Forge* he describes an old-fashioned blacksmith in a leather apron, surrounded by 'old axles and iron hoops' that are rusting; the traffic that passes by produces 'a clatter of hoofs', not the roar of tractors. Heaney admires the skill and artistry of the craftsmen, such as the thatcher who turns up unexpectedly on his bicycle, and the water diviner whose hazel stick would react to the presence of water when he himself held it but remained 'dead' in the grasp of bystanders who tried to imitate him; Heaney also writes of his mother's skill as she makes the decisive first turn of the butter-churn in the long process that laboriously turns buttermilk into yellow butter.

Heaney admires the old-fashioned virtues that his father and grandfather displayed in running their farm:

> 'By God, the old man could handle a spade.
> Just like his old man.
> My grandfather cut more turf in a day
> Than any other man on Toner's bog.'

Consequently he resolves to demonstrate as a writer the honesty, integrity and conscientiousness that his father and grandfather displayed as hard-working farmers:

> 'Between my finger and my thumb
> The squat pen rests.
> I'll dig with it.'

Heaney responds creatively and positively to the genuine feelings that warm the lives of the characters in his rural landscape. *Honeymoon Flight* brings to life the loving trust between husband and wife setting out on their honeymoon; in *Valediction*, a lover realises how the absence of the woman he loves may rob his life of its essential motivation; *The Wife's Tale* reveals the wife's pride in the confidence with which her husband had grown the corn and then organised the men who harvested it.

In the civil war that has raged in Northern Ireland for most of Heaney's life, he clearly sides with the Catholic separatists. He has become an Irish citizen and has insisted in a recent poem that 'My passport's green. No glass of ours was ever raised to toast the Queen.' He blames the Irish and British governments for failing to solve Ireland's political and religious problems. In thinking about these problems he displays only resignation, stoicism and a deep pessimism. His poem *Derry Images 1968–71* emphasises the precarious and poverty-stricken side of Londonderry, with only jerry-built houses ever being erected in the Catholic areas, and violence still breaking out among the visible reminders of the siege of 1689, when the Irish Catholics (with French help) besieged the Protestant defenders for one hundred and five days. Heaney tells the story of the Protestant painter who, in the early 1960s, could call on a Catholic friend to set and paint his railings. Ireland's enduring tragedy is marked by the fact that Protestants and Catholics have made far fewer friendly gestures to one another since the late 1960s, when violence of all kinds broke out again. Heaney's poem *Getting on on the Railways* suggests how much harm is done to Irish railways by the selfish grasping of various groups of skilled workers, whose skills are often minimal, but whose unions grab for them a bigger and bigger share of the available money.

But Heaney declares his allegiances most openly when he is describing past events, such as when the Croppies, the rustics armed with pikes and scythes who died 'shaking scythes at cannon', were mown down by the professional British artillerymen in the battle of Vinegar Hill, which brought to a disastrous and bloody end the hopeless Irish Rebellion of 1798. Similarly Heaney shows on which side his sympathy lies in *For the Commander of the Eliza*: ironically the narrator condemns those English officials who 'urged free relief for famine victims' during the Potato Famine of the 1840s; they did not realise how hard a battle they needed to fight to convince their political masters that relief on this scale was necessary.

The historian G. M. Trevelyan has said that 'the sentimental feud that still divides Ireland' came to life again in what is fundamentally its modern form as a result of the religious rising of the Irish rebels who were so easily and bloodily defeated at Vinegar Hill. So Heaney was right to realise that the Croppies of the late eighteenth century were decisively recommencing the political and religious rivalry that has brought so much violence to Ireland in the last twenty years.

In *North* and some of his later volumes such as *Field Work* (1979) and *Preoccupations: Selected Prose* 1968–78 ((1980), Heaney has found an oblique way of commenting on current events by studying the archaeology that has found well-preserved corpses of men and women in the peat bogs of Ireland and Denmark. Firstly, these provide Ireland with a new mythology, because Ireland owes so much of its cultural origins to the raiders who sailed their longships to Dublin and other Viking ports. Secondly, many of the dead whose corpses have been dug up by archaeologists were obviously victims of ritual killings. So Heaney sees a direct similarity between their fates and those of the modern victims of sectarian killings; hence his interest in the buried corpse of the Grabaulle Man:

> 'As if he had been poured
> In tar, he lies
> on a pillow of turf
> and seems to weep
> The black river of himself.'

At later periods in his life Heaney has visited and lived in various islands off the west coast of Ireland, and his knowledge of these islands contributes another thread to his poetry, as in this image of the Aran islands:

> 'The timeless waves, bright sifting, broken glass.
> Came dazzling around, into the rocks,
> Came glinting, sifting from the Americas . . .'

In conclusion, what Heaney contributes to his study of people and events in Irish politics and Irish farming is his unflagging sense of rhythm and his gift for choosing clear, honest words. He looks at an Irish farm or an Irish landscape without being tempted to repeat the phrases and rhythms of any other poets, so his poetry has the qualities of freshness and vitality that so many critics have rightly detected in it. Our innate interest in farming may be slight, but Heaney awakens our senses by his use of striking phrases such as 'the hum and gulp' of the threshing machine, or 'the dark drop, the trapped sky, the smells of waterweed' that he sees in a well, or the dead turkeys that lie on cold marble slabs 'in immodest underwear frills of feather'. Phrases such as these brilliantly evoke the physical conditions that Heaney is remembering. Heaney himself has compared this craft of putting feelings into words to divination, the craft by which the water diviner discovers water that is hidden; Heaney also believes that writing poetry is similar to archaeological digging which 'can let down a shaft into real life'.

Heaney has said that he began to write poetry successfully in his early twenties when he began to teach. In order to pass on the knowledge he had about the traditional farming methods that survived in rural Ireland, he had to deepen that knowledge and in the process find out more about himself: writing poetry proved to be an effective method of doing this. At the same time he discovered a useful model in Ted Hughes – a contemporary poet who wrote realistically about the everyday experiences of rural life. Heaney could learn from Hughes' direct style without imitating his subject matter too closely; there was just sufficient similarity between rural Ireland and the semi-rural West Riding that Ted Hughes described at the beginning of his career.

Trout

Hangs, a fat gun-barrel,
deep under arched bridges
or slips like butter down
the throat of the river.

From depths smooth-skinned as plums
his muzzle gets bull's eye;
picks off grass-seed and moths
that vanish, torpedoed,

Where water unravels
over gravel-beds he
is fired from the shallows
white belly reporting

flat; darts like a tracer-
bullet back between stones
and is never burnt out.
A volley of cold blood

ramrodding the current.

The Wife's Tale

When I had spread it all on linen cloth
Under the hedge, I called them over.
The hum and gulp of the thresher ran down
And the big belt slewed to a standstill, straw
Hanging undelivered in the jaws.
There was such quiet that I heard their boots
Crunching the stubble twenty yards away.

He lay down and said 'Give these fellows theirs.
I'm in no hurry,' plucking grass in handfuls
And tossing it in the air. 'That looks well.'
(He nodded at my white cloth on the grass.)

'I declare a woman could lay out a field
Though boys like us have little call for cloths.'
He winked, then watched me as I poured a cup
And buttered the thick slices that he likes.
'It's threshing better than I thought, and mind
It's good clean seed. Away over there and look.'
Always this inspection has to be made
Even when I don't know what to look for.

But I ran my hand in the half-filled bags
Hooked to the slots. It was hard as shot,
Innumerable and cool. The bags gaped
Where the chutes ran back to the stilled drum
And forks were stuck at angles in the ground
As javelins might mark lost battlefields.
I moved between them back across the stubble.

They lay in the ring of their own crusts and dregs
Smoking and saying nothing. 'There's good yield,
Isn't there?' – as proud as if he were the land itself –
'Enough for crushing and for sowing both.'
And that was it. I'd come and he had shown me
So I belonged no further to the work.
I gathered cups and folded up the cloth
And went. But they still kept their ease
Spread out, unbuttoned, grateful, under the trees.

SEAMUS HEANEY

Churning Day

A thick crust, coarse-grained as limestone rough-cast,
hardened gradually on top of the four crocks
that stood, large pottery bombs, in the small pantry.
After the hot brewery of gland, cud and udder
cool porous earthenware fermented the buttermilk
for churning day, when the hooped churn was scoured
with plumping kettles and the busy scrubber
echoed daintily on the seasoned wood.
It stood then, purified, on the flagged kitchen floor.

Out came the four crocks, spilled their heavy lip
of cream, their white insides, into the sterile churn.
The staff, like a great whisky muddler fashioned
in deal wood, was plunged in, the lid fitted.
My mother took first turn, set up rhythms
that slugged and thumped for hours. Arms ached.
Hands blistered. Cheeks and clothes were spattered
with flabby milk.

Where finally gold flecks
began to dance. They poured hot water then,
sterilized a birchwood-bowl
and little corrugated butter-spades.
Their short stroke quickened, suddenly
a yellow curd was weighting the churned up white,
heavy and rich, coagulated sunlight
that they fished, dripping, in a wide tin strainer,
heaped up like gilded gravel in the bowl.

The house would stink long after churning day,
acrid as a sulphur mine. The empty crocks
were ranged along the wall again, the butter
in soft printed slabs was piled on pantry shelves.
And in the house we moved with gravid ease,
our brains turned crystals full of clean deal churns,
the plash and gurgle of the sour-breathed milk,
the pat and slap of small spades on wet lumps.

Rookery

Here they come, freckling the sunset,
The slow big sailers bearing down
On the plantation. They have flown
Their sorties and are now well met.

The upper twigs dip and wobble
With each almost two-point landing,
Then ride to rest. There is nothing
Else to do now only settle.

But they keep up a guttural chat
As stragglers knock the roost see-saw.
Something's satisfied in that caw.
Who wouldn't come to rest like that?

Thatcher

Bespoke for weeks, he turned up some morning
Unexpectedly, his bicycle slung
With a light ladder and a bag of knives.
He eyed the old rigging, poked at the eaves,

Opened and handled sheaves of lashed wheat-straw.
Next, the bundled rods: hazel and willow
Were flicked for weight, twisted in case they'd snap.
It seemed he spent the morning warming up:

Then fixed the ladder, laid out well honed blades
And snipped at straw and sharpened ends of rods
That, bent in two, made a white-pronged staple
For pinning down his world, handful by handful.

Couchant for days on sods above the rafters
He shaved and flushed the butts, stitched all together
Into a sloped honeycomb, a stubble patch,
And left them gaping at his Midas touch.

SEAMUS HEANEY

Digging

Between my finger and my thumb
The squat pen rests; snug as a gun.

Under my window, a clean rasping sound
When the spade sinks into gravelly ground:
My father, digging. I look down

Till his straining rump among the flowerbeds
Bends low, comes up twenty years away
Stooping in rhythm through potato drills
Where he was digging.

The coarse boot nestled on the lug, the shaft
Against the inside knee was levered firmly.
He rooted out tall tops, buried the bright edge deep
To scatter new potatoes that we picked
Loving their cool hardness in our hands.

By God, the old man could handle a spade.
Just like his old man.

My grandfather cut more turf in a day
Than any other man on Toner's bog.
Once I carried him milk in a bottle
Corked sloppily with paper. He straightened up
To drink it, then fell to right away

Nicking and slicing neatly, heaving sods
Over his shoulder, going down and down
For the good turf. Digging.

The cold smell of potato mould, the squelch and slap
Of soggy peat, the curt cuts of an edge
Through living roots awaken in my head.
But I've no spade to follow men like them.

Between my finger and my thumb
The squat pen rests.
I'll dig with it.

Storm on the Island

We are prepared: we build our houses squat,
Sink walls in rock and roof them with good slate.
This wizened earth has never troubled us
With hay, so, as you see, there are no stacks
Or stooks that can be lost. Nor are there trees
Which might prove company when it blows full
Blast: you know what I mean – leaves and branches
Can raise a tragic chorus in a gale
So that you listen to the thing you fear
Forgetting that it pummels your house too.
But there are no trees, no natural shelter.
You might think that the sea is company,
Exploding comfortably down on the cliffs
But no: when it begins, the flung spray hits
The very windows, spits like a tame cat
Turned savage. We just sit tight while wind dives
And strafes invisibly. Space is a salvo,
We are bombarded by the empty air.
Strange, it is a huge nothing that we fear.

The Diviner

Cut from the green hedge a forked hazel stick
That he held tight by the arms of the V:
Circling the terrain, hunting the pluck
Of water, nervous, but professionally

Unfussed. The pluck came sharp as a sting.
The rod jerked down with precise convulsions,
Spring water suddenly broadcasting
Through a green aerial its secret stations.

The bystanders would ask to have a try.
He handed them the rod without a word.
It lay dead in their grasp till nonchalantly
He gripped expectant wrists. The hazel stirred.

Valediction

Lady with the frilled blouse
And simple tartan skirt,
Since you have left the house
Its emptiness has hurt
All thought. In your presence
Time rode easy, anchored
On a smile; but absence
Rocked love's balance, unmoored
The days. They buck and bound
Across the calendar
Pitched from the quiet sound
Of your flower-tender
Voice. Need breaks on my strand;
You've gone, I am at sea.
Until you resume command
Self is in mutiny.

Honeymoon Flight

Below, the patchwork earth, dark hems of hedge,
The long grey tapes of road that bind and loose
Villages and fields in casual marriage:
We bank above the small lough and farmhouse

And the sure green world goes topsy-turvy
As we climb out of our familiar landscape.
The engine noises change. You look at me.
The coastline slips away beneath the wing-tip.

And launched right off the earth by force of fire
We hang, miraculous, above the water,
Dependent on the invisible air
To keep us airborne and to bring us further.

Ahead of us the sky's a geyser now.
A calm voice talks of cloud yet we feel lost.
Air-pockets jolt our fears and down we go.
Travellers, at this point, can only trust.

SEAMUS HEANEY

Getting on on the Railways

There's few but me's just plain goods-porter here.
Soon as you've to read labels to know where
to hump the stuff they're tied to, grade goes up:
special abilities. 'Sides, there's other things.

Take the motormen, allus arguing
with the men who load the trailers for their rounds,
how all's in the wrong order to pull off.
Both once were graded checkers. Motormen
got together, stuck out for how they must
get made up senior checkers so they can
bollocks the loaders, call them every name
under the sun like they do anyway,
but by rights, for stacking trailers wrong.
Next the loaders found out that the forms
they list the goods on aren't straightforward forms,
oh no, they're multiple, carbons and all.
That entitled them to upgrading too.
So the motormen are back at square one. It'll
go on till they're all station managers.
They'd still waste half the morning arguing.

Another case: old Greg who checks out stock
in the Order Shed, he's not allowed to lift,
that's why they gave him that job. Can't hold owt,
poor old Gregory, not even his beer,
really shouldn't be working, no, the only
place for him is six foot under. Well,
he got so much wrong counting cartons out
they made him up a grade to give him an
increased sense of responsibility.
So now he draws more doing more things wrong.
Wrecking the bloody railways'd take him to
the big boss seat. He'd not be first, at that.

Requiem for the Croppies

The pockets of our greatcoats full of barley –
No kitchens on the run, no striking camp –
We moved quick and sudden in our own country.
The priest lay behind ditches with the tramp.
A people, hardly marching – on the hike –
We found new tactics happening each day:
We'd cut through reins and rider with the pike
And stampede cattle into infantry,
Then retreat through hedges where cavalry must be thrown.
Until, on Vinegar Hill, the fatal conclave.
Terraced thousands died, shaking scythes at cannon.
The hillside blushes, soaked in our broken wave.
They buried us without shroud or coffin
And in August the barley grew up out of the grave.

TED HUGHES

Ted Hughes was born in 1930 at Mytholmroyd, a little town in West Yorkshire in the valley of the River Calder. It was an area similar to the part of Nottinghamshire where D. H. Lawrence was born. There were mills and factories and coal-pits, most of which were ugly, but there were no large towns, so that much unspoilt or half-spoilt countryside survived in between the factories and houses.

Hughes' father was a carpenter. He often spoke of his grim experiences in World War I, and stimulated in his son an intense interest in this war. His stories provided Hughes with the material for several effective poems, such as *Six Young Men.*

The weather, the people and the animals of this Pennine area also fascinated Ted Hughes as a boy, and they provided him with a unique subject-matter for the poetry that he was to write as a grown man. In particular, he became an expert on animals. When he was three he could extend his toy lead animals all round the fender. When he was a few years older he would capture live mice, shoot rabbits and study the dead owls and magpies that met a variety of deaths, from being shot by his elder brother to dying of cold.

As a boy he went to Mexborough Grammar School (because his family had moved to another part of Yorkshire), and he then won a scholarship to Pembroke College, Cambridge, though he had first to serve for two years in the RAF as a wireless mechanic.

After obtaining a degree, Ted Hughes worked at jobs of a type that few graduates seek. For instance, he was a rose-gardener, then a night-watchman in a steel factory, and later on did the washing-up in a café that was part of London Zoo.

In 1956 he married Sylvia Plath, the American poet, and became a schoolteacher. At first all went well. He published two volumes of poetry (*The Hawk in the Rain*, 1957, and *Lupercal*, 1960) and they were warmly received by most reviewers. Meanwhile Sylvia Plath's poetry also won acclaim. In 1962, however, Hughes and his wife parted, and in 1963 she committed suicide. This tragedy had a stunning effect on Hughes and it was eight years before he published his next volume of poetry, *Crow*. His earlier volumes had won praise for the striking poems about predatory animals and birds, notably hawks and buzzards. For instance, he described in admiring tones the jaguar in the zoo who remained defiant and mesmerised the human onlookers as he strode up and down. To express his admiration for these violent and vital beings, Hughes developed a forceful style of writing, and used comparisons that are surprising, sardonic and witty. For example, he stretches the usual meaning of the nouns *sophistry* and *manners* when he expresses the boastings of his Hawk in these words:

> 'There is no sophistry in my body:
> My manners are tearing off heads . . .'

When Hughes describes pike he helps create his impression of their forcefulness and greed by using unusual verbs: green is *tigering* the gold, the fishes' gills are *kneading* quietly, and the deep pond left behind by the monks has *stilled* legendary depths. Similarly Hughes' thistles *spike* the summer air, while the metallic grey woods of leafless November are *treed* with iron. Like Dick Straightup (the strong old man in the village pub whom he idolises), Hughes finds words that *tug up the bottom-most stones* of the Pennine village that he remembers from his boyhood. His reading of the poetry of Gerard Manley Hopkins and Dylan Thomas encouraged him to use in his verse the homely, lively rhythms of conversation that he found among the country people in the West Riding. Certainly one of Hughes' virtues as a poet is his gift for using rhythms that suggest the distinctive movements of individual animals or birds and also imply the desolate unhappiness of some human beings.

Like many poets Hughes is at his best when he writes unselfconsciously about his childhood experiences. Just as Wordsworth wrote best about his childhood reactions to Nature when skating on the ice of Lake Windermere or rowing a stolen boat at night on Ullswater, so Hughes makes constant references in his best poetry to the West Yorkshire of his youth.

His most convincing descriptions of people are of those whom he remembers from his own past, such as Dick Straightup and the retired Colonel. Similarly his poem *The Wind* is a brilliant picture of the house on the windy Pennine ridge where his parents lived when he was a boy. The house is like a ship at sea:

> 'The house has been far out at sea all night,
> The woods crashing through darkness, the
>   booming hills,
> Winds stampeding the fields under the window
>   ....'

His poem *The Horses* describes the contrast between the animals as they seemed just *before* and just *after* dawn when Hughes watched them on an early morning walk in West Yorkshire countryside. The poem ends with Hughes hoping that when in the future he is in noisy, busy towns he will keep alive his memory of 'so lonely a place – Between the streams and the red clouds'.

Even his poetry about World War I is chiefly about West Yorkshire's memories and mementoes of its dead from that war.

A difficult question to answer is whether Hughes' earlier poems use animals as symbols or are really straightforward poems about animals and birds. For example, is *The Hawk Roosting* a poem about a hawk or about a man (or mankind) in a predatory mood? Probably Hughes' best poems are the most straightforward, where he is writing with sincere respect for an animal or bird as a being in its own right, and is respecting the vitality that that creature displays more clearly or consistently than civilised people do.

Hughes has protested against the falsity of contrived interpretations of his poems that label the roosting hawk as a 'fascist' or as a 'symbol of some horrible totalitarian dictator'.

However, Hughes' volume of poems intended for adults, *Crow*, shocked many of his admirers. (This present anthology includes only two poems from this collection – *Crow Hears Fate Knock on the Door* and *Dawn's Rose*.) Many readers argued that the poems in *Crow* were an exaggerated caricature of the previous poem *Hawk Roosting*, where the hawk says: 'it took the whole of Creation to produce my foot'; in the later book of poems Crow speaks as though he was the collaborator of the Creator. Moreover Crow, the narrator or speaker in the poems, overuses new tricks of style, such as putting many lines in capital letters and using short stanzas which only fill up one or two lines and do not even finish sentences.

When *The Times Literary Supplement* reviewed *Crow* it did so under the headline *A mouthful of blood*. It accused Hughes of 'a vague, simple-mindedly asserted preference for the primitive, the brutal and the sudden'. It argued that since Hughes had already written about most known animals he was now inventing imaginary ones to write about or was writing second poems about old favourites. Crow, the reviewer continued, enjoyed moving in a world that was 'drenched in blood, racked with agony, and devastated by numerous varieties of violence'.

In reality Hughes was merely trying to experiment with a new style, so he wrote poems such as a crow, with its unmusical voice and carnivorous habits, might be expected to compose. But Hughes then went further and depicted the crow as one of the most intelligent and widely distributed birds. He began to include in his poetry references to the parts that crows play in the fairy stories of various races, and to the Celtic belief in the death-goddess who looked like a crow. But many of the Crow poems puzzled their readers by assuming that they had more knowledge of Celtic mythology than the poems explained. Moreover there was too much similarity of mood between the poems and they lacked any beauty in their sounds and images. Even Crow was made to despair when he saw the ugly mess that people's litter has made of the earth:

> 'He saw this shoe, with no sole, rain-sodden,
> lying on a moor.
> And there was this garbage can, bottom rusted
> away,
> A playing place for the wind, in a waste of
> puddles.'

In other poems, however, Hughes gives Crow the sort of role that many mythologies give to the Devil or the Trickster, who is a clown figure working in continuous opposition to the Creator.

Nevertheless Hughes' later poems, published after Crow (e.g. *Season Songs*), present his readers with a much wider choice of topics and of styles, and with a more contented, optimistic view of the future. For instance, *Five Birds in Paradise* introduces us to five different birds and thereby produces five poems in different moods. Again, *Snow and Snow* invites us to enjoy the brilliance of the morning sunlight after the first snowfall of the winter.

In the late 1970s Hughes published two collections of poetry, *Moortown* and *Remains of Elmet*; he also contributed twelve new poems to Michael Morpurgo's *All Around the Year*, and in 1981 he published *Under the North Star*. Elmet was the name of the British kingdom in West Yorkshire which included Hughes' native district and which resisted conquest by the Anglo-Saxons for some time after the rest of Yorkshire had been overrun. In his book on Elmet, Hughes includes black and white photographs by Fay Godwin; he uses both the photographs and his own prose comments to underline the main point of his poems – that the appearance of the area has changed very decisively in recent times. For instance, he says: 'Throughout my lifetime, since 1930, I have watched the mills of the region and their attendant chapels die. Within the last fifteen years the end has come. They are now virtually dead, and the population of the valley and its hillsides, so rooted for so long, is changing rapidly.'

However, Hughes' latest publications contain many poems about animals, which continue to show the same sympathy for animals that he always felt. Though many of these later poems are almost a didactic lesson on how to look after animals well, they still record in a dramatic, poetic way the unique moments of an animal's life. The style of these later poems has become less brilliant and compelling than in the best of his early poems, but it is far less macabre and exaggerated and repetitive than it was in *Crow*. Consequently, if we look at the whole sweep of Hughes' poetry and do not fasten our attention too narrowly on *Crow*, then we shall welcome Hughes' very personal and distinctive contributions to modern poetry; in doing this we shall respond more to the potent life-force in his poems than to the violence. We shall see the force of Hughes' own defence of himself: 'My poems are not about violence but vitality.' Hughes believes that the hypocrisy and convention of modern life have hidden the vitality which we ought to feel, and which the animals and birds whom he admires still display. In writing about these animals and birds he tries to teach us more about our essential selves. Moreover, at his best he registers the fascination and awe that animals and birds evoke from him – not mere despair.

Of all the poets who are included in this anthology, Hughes is the one who does most to fulfil the old-fashioned role of the poet – that of inspiring his readers. He feels the importance of the life-forces that we share with birds and animals, and does his best to make us more aware of them. He conveys their forcefulness by his defiant exaggeration and striking metaphors. Consequently, as Keith Sagar wrote in *The Art of Ted Hughes*: 'The poems crackle with surplus energy. The words leap off the page to grapple or strike the reader.'

For these reasons his appointment as Poet Laureate was warmly welcomed in 1984. It was realised that his poetry is always honest and forceful and modern.

Hawk Roosting

I sit in the top of the wood, my eyes closed.
Inaction, no falsifying dream
Between my hooked head and hooked feet:
Or in sleep rehearse perfect kills and eat.

The convenience of the high trees!
The air's buoyancy and the sun's ray
Are of advantage to me;
And the earth's face upward for my inspection.

My feet are locked upon the rough bark.
It took the whole of Creation
To produce my foot, my each feather:
Now I hold Creation in my foot

Or fly up, and revolve it all slowly –
I kill where I please because it is all mine.
There is no sophistry in my body:
My manners are tearing off heads –

The allotment of death.
For the one path of my flight is direct
Through the bones of the living.
No arguments assert my right:

The sun is behind me.
Nothing has changed since I began.
My eye has permitted no change.
I am going to keep things like this.

Pike

Pike, three inches long, perfect
Pike in all parts, green tigering the gold.
Killers from the egg: the malevolent aged grin.
They dance on the surface among the flies.

Or move, stunned by their own grandeur,
Over a bed of emerald, silhouette
Of submarine delicacy and horror.
A hundred feet long in their world.

In ponds, under the heat-struck lily pads –
Gloom of their stillness:
Logged on last year's black leaves, watching upwards.
Or hung in an amber cavern of weeds

The jaws' hooked clamp and fangs
Not to be changed at this date;
A life subdued to its instrument;
The gills kneading quietly, and the pectorals.

Three we kept behind glass,
Jungled in weed: three inches, four,
And four and a half: fed fry to them –
Suddenly there were two. Finally one

With a sag belly and the grin it was born with.
And indeed they spare nobody.
Two, six pounds each, over two feet long,
High and dry and dead in the willow-herb –

One jammed past its gills down the other's gullet:
The outside eye stared: as a vice locks –
The same iron in this eye
Though its film shrank in death.

A pond I fished, fifty yard across,
Whose lilies and muscular tench
Had outlasted every visible stone
Of the monastery that planted them –

Stilled legendary depth:
It was as deep as England. It held
Pike too immense to stir, so immense and old
That past nightfall I dared not cast

But silently cast and fished
With the hair frozen on my head
For what might move, for what eye might move.
The still splashes on the dark pond,

Owls hushing the floating woods
Frail on my ear against the dream
Darkness beneath night's darkness had freed,
That rose slowly towards me, watching.

Thistles

Against the rubber tongues of cows and the hoeing hands of
men
Thistles spike the summer air
Or crackle open under a blue-black pressure.

Every one a revengeful burst
Of resurrection, a grasped fistful
Of splintered weapons and Icelandic frost thrust up

From the underground stain of a decayed Viking.
They are like pale hair and the gutturals of dialects.
Every one manages a plume of blood.

Then they grow grey like men.
Mown down, it is a feud. Their sons appear,
Stiff with weapons, fighting back over the same ground.

Crow Hears Fate Knock on the Door

Crow looked at the world, mountainously heaped.
He looked at the heavens, littering away
Beyond every limit.
He looked in front of his feet at the little stream
Chugging on like an auxiliary motor
Fastened to this infinite engine.

He imagined the whole engineering
Of its assembly, repairs and maintenance –
And felt helpless.

He plucked grass-heads and gazed into them
Waiting for first instructions.
He studied a stone from the stream.
He found a dead mole and slowly he took it apart
Then stared at the gobbets, feeling helpless.
He walked, he walked
Letting the translucent starry spaces
Blow in his ear cluelessly.

Yet the prophecy inside him, like a grimace,
Was I WILL MEASURE IT ALL AND OWN IT ALL
AND I WILL BE INSIDE IT
AS INSIDE MY OWN LAUGHTER
AND NOT STARING OUT AT IT THROUGH WALLS
OR MY EYE'S COLD QUARANTINE
FROM A BURIED CELL OF BLOODY BLACKNESS –
This prophecy was inside him, like a steel spring
Slowly rending the vital fibres.

Dawn's Rose

Is melting an old frost moon.

Agony under agony, the quiet of dust,
And a crow talking to stony skylines.

Desolate is the crow's puckered cry
As an old woman's mouth
When the eyelids have finished
And the hills continue.

A cry
Wordless
As the newborn baby's grieving
On the steely scales.

As the dull gunshot and its after-râle
Among conifers, in rainy twilight.

Or the suddenly dropped, heavily dropped
Star of blood on the fat leaf.

Snow and Snow

Snow is sometimes a she, a soft one.
  Her kiss on your cheek, her finger on your sleeve
In early December, on a warm evening,
  And you turn to meet her, saying "It's snowing!"
    But it is not. And nobody's there.
    Empty and calm is the air.

Sometimes the snow is a he, a sly one.
  Weakly he signs the dry stone with a damp spot.
Waifish he floats and touches the pond and is not.
  Treacherous-beggarly he falters, and taps at the window
    A little longer he clings to the grass-blade tip
    Getting his grip.

Then how she leans, how furry foxwrap she nestles
  The sky with her warm, and the earth with her softness.
How her lit crowding fairytales sink through the space-silence
  To build her palace, till it twinkles in starlight –
    Too frail for a foot
    Or a crumb of soot.

Then how his muffled armies move in all night
  And we wake and every road is blockaded
Every hill taken and every farm occupied
  And the white glare of his tents is on the ceiling.
    And all that dull blue day and on into the gloaming
    We have to watch more coming.

Then everything in the rubbish-heaped world
  Is a bridesmaid at her miracle.
Dunghills and crumbly dark old barns are bowed in the chapel
      of her sparkle,
  The gruesome boggy cellars of the wood
    Are a wedding of lace
    Now taking place.

The Horses

I climbed through woods in the hour-before-dawn dark.
Evil air, a frost-making stillness,

Not a leaf, not a bird, –
A world cast in frost. I came out above the wood

Where my breath left tortuous statues in the iron light.
But the valleys were draining the darkness

Till the moorline – blackening dregs of the brightening grey –
Halved the sky ahead. And I saw the horses:

Huge in the dense grey – ten together –
Megalith-still. They breathed, making no move,

With draped manes and tilted hind-hooves,
Making no sound.

I passed: not one snorted or jerked its head.
Grey silent fragments

Of a grey silent world.

I listened in emptiness on the moor-ridge.
The curlew's tear turned its edge on the silence.

Slowly detail leafed from the darkness. Then the sun
Orange, red, red erupted

Silently, and splitting to its core tore and flung cloud,
Shook the gulf open, showed blue,

And the big planets hanging –
I turned

Stumbling in the fever of a dream, down towards
The dark woods, from the kindling tops,

And came to the horses.
  There, still they stood,
But now steaming and glistening under the flow of light,

Their draped stone manes, their tilted hind-hooves
Stirring under a thaw while all around them

The frost showed its fires. But still they made no sound.
Not one snorted or stamped,

Their hung heads patient as the horizons,
High over valleys, in the red levelling rays –

In din of the crowded streets, going among the years, the faces,
May I still meet my memory in so lonely a place

Between the streams and the red clouds, hearing curlews,
Hearing the horizons endure.

TED HUGHES

The Warm and the Cold

Freezing dusk is closing
  Like a slow trap of steel
On trees and roads and hills and all
  That can no longer feel.
    But the carp is in its depth
      Like a planet in its heaven
    And the badger in its bedding
      Like a loaf in the oven
    And the butterfly in its mummy
      Like a viol in its case
    And the owl in its feathers
      Like a doll in its lace.

Freezing dusk has tightened
  Like a nut screwed tight
On the starry aeroplane
  Of the hurtling night.
    But the trout is in its hole
      Like a giggle in a sleeper.
    The hare strays down the highway
      Like a root going deeper.
    The snail is dry in the outhouse
      Like a seed in a sunflower.
    The owl is pale on the gatepost
      Like a clock on its tower.

Moonlight freezes the shaggy world
  Like a mammoth of ice –
The past and the future
  Are the jaws of a steel vice.
    But the cod is in the tide-rip
      Like a key in a purse.
    The deer are on the bare-blown hill
      Like smiles on a nurse.
    The flies are behind the plaster
      Like the lost score of a jig
    Sparrows are in the ivy-clump
      Like money in a pig.

Such a frost
   The freezing moon
      Has lost her wits.

A star falls.

The sweating farmers
   Turn in their sleep
      Like oxen on spits.

The Retired Colonel

Who lived at the top end of our street
Was a Mafeking stereotype, ageing.
Came, face pulped scarlet with kept rage,
For air past our gate.
Barked at his dog knout and whipcrack
And cowerings of India: five or six wars
Stiffened in his reddened neck;
Brow bull-down for the stroke.

Wife dead, daughters gone, lived on
Honouring his own caricature.
Shot through the heart with whisky wore
The lurch like ancient courage, would not go down

While posterity's trash stood, held
His habits like a last stand, even
As if he had Victoria rolled
In a Union Jack in that stronghold.
And what if his sort should vanish?
The rabble starlings roar upon
Trafalgar. The man-eating British lion
By a pimply age brought down.
Here's his head mounted, though only in rhymes,
Beside the head of the last English
Wolf (those starved gloomy times!)
And the last sturgeon of Thames.

Mill Ruins

One morning
The shuttle's spirit failed to come back
(Japan had trapped it
In a reconstructed loom
Cribbed from smiling fools in Todmorden.)

Cloth rotted, in spite of the nursing.
Its great humming abbeys became tombs.

And the children
Of rock and water and a draughty absence
Of everything else
Roaming for leftovers.

Smashed all that would smash
What would not smash they burned
What would not burn

They levered loose and toppled down hillsides

Then trailed away homeward aimlessly
Like the earliest
Homeless Norsemen.

Six Young Men

The celluloid of a photograph holds them well –
Six young men, familiar to their friends.
Four decades that have faded and ochre-tinged
This photograph have not wrinkled the faces or the hands.
Though their cocked hats are not now fashionable,
Their shoes shine. One imparts an intimate smile,
One chews a grass, one lowers his eyes, bashful,
One is ridiculous with cocky pride –
Six months after this picture they all were dead.

All are trimmed for a Sunday jaunt. I know
That bilberried bank, that thick tree, that black wall,
Which are there yet and not changed. From where these sit
You hear the water of seven streams fall
To the roarer in the bottom, and through all
The leafy valley a rumouring of air go.
Pictured here, their expressions listen yet,
And still that valley has not changed its sound
Though their faces are four decades under the ground.

This one was shot in an attack and lay
Calling in the wire, then this one, his best friend,
Went out to bring him in and was shot too;
And this one, the very moment he was warned
From potting at tin-cans in no-man's land,
Fell back dead with his rifle-sights shot away.
The rest, nobody knows what they came to,
But come to the worst they must have done, and held it
Closer than their hope; all were killed.

Here, see a man's photograph,
The locket of a smile, turned overnight
Into the hospital of his mangled last
Agony and hours; see bundled in it
His mightier-than-a-man dead bulk and weight:
And on this one place which keeps him alive
(In his Sunday best) see fall war's worst
Thinkable flash and rending, onto his smile
Forty years rotting into soil.

That man's not more alive whom you confront
And shake by the hand, see hale, hear speak loud,
Than any of these six celluloid smiles are,
Nor prehistoric or fabulous beast more dead;
No thought so vivid as their smoking blood:
To regard this photograph might well dement,
Such contradictory permanent horrors here
Smile from the single exposure and shoulder out
One's own body from its instant and heat.

ELIZABETH JENNINGS

Elizabeth Jennings was born in Boston, Lincolnshire in 1926. She was educated at St Anne's College, Oxford and later worked as a librarian and as a publisher's reader. Her poems won fame at once, and she was one of the poets represented in *Penguin Modern Poets 1*. Later her *Collected Works* were published by Macmillan.

In 1956 Robert Conquest edited an anthology called *New Lines*, which represented the work of poets who had turned their backs on both the romanticism of Dylan Thomas and the obscurity of T. S. Eliot, and who were consequently much easier to understand. They took a cool, straight look at modern life. They portrayed it in clear pictures that were both comprehensible and objective. Conquest included Elizabeth Jennings among these poets, who became known to literary critics as 'The Movement'. But she herself was quick to point out that whereas the other poets in this collection wrote from an objective, almost sceptical and agnostic point of view, she has always been a committed and convinced Roman Catholic. 'My Roman Catholic religion and my poems,' she insisted, 'are the most important things in my life.' Certainly she has continued to write many poems that express her devotional approach, such as her poem about the Roman Church of St Paul outside the City Walls, where for her 'prayer comes quicker than an act'.

Elizabeth Jennings has also written some convincing and sensitive love poetry. The quiet effectiveness with which she describes the ways in which love-affairs can fail never sinks into self-pity and she retains a subdued dignity in recording her disappointments.

She has written some very realistic portraits of members of her own family and writes very effective poems about the problems and misunderstandings of family life. The way in which she hurt her grandmother by refusing to go out with her when she was a child reminds us of the ways in which we unintentionally hurt members of our own families.

She writes more about the emotions between members of

families than about the tangible circumstances of a modern household. But she covers a wide variety of subject matter in her poems, writing on topics as various as the painter Rembrandt, the contentment of her own grandmother in old age, and the uncommon meanings that lovers can put into common words such as 'Your turn'. Much that she writes is in the conventional iambic metre of most traditional English poetry and she usually uses rhyme, though her rhymes include the half-rhymes that Wilfred Owen used in some of his poetry about World War I. What is modern about her poetry is her consistent use of the natural, English word that fits the context, her avoidance of all literary language, the fact that her poems are quite unlike those of any other poet, and the intensity of her resolve to be truthful and clear. She gives us an honest account of the life she has led and a credible picture of the people and places that she has known.

Elizabeth Jennings has interested herself in what Tony Connor called 'the tricky district' of the mind, especially her own mind which she continues to explore in repeated studies of gentle self-discovery. She also explores other people's states of mind, especially within her own family; for instance she is as interested in what grandparents think of their grandchildren as in what grandchildren think of their grandparents.

She has claimed that whereas 'Prose has always seemed to me an attempt to find words for something which I already know,' her best poems are those which 'manage to say in a strict inevitable form something that I did not know before.' She has found out more about her own emotions and states of mind by writing poems about them.

She is a poet who has been content to keep writing the sort of poem that she knows she will always write well. Although she takes the risk of writing poems that could be over-similar, she does produce just enough variations to avoid monotony. Kenneth Allott has summed her up wittily: 'What I value best in Miss Jennings's poems is their courtesy to the reader in their assumption that he is intelligently wide awake and does not need to be bawled at – at moments I have felt appreciatively that she probably washes her hands and puts on new white gloves before she starts to write.' But this witticism suggests that Elizabeth Jennings is reluctant to face unpleasant truths. This is an unfair criticism because as a poet she is certainly capable of putting a world of psychological truth into a short, simple poem. It is surprising how much she can tell us about human nature in a few lines.

The Young Ones

They slip on to the bus, hair piled up high.
New styles each month, it seems to me. I look,
Not wanting to be seen, casting my eye
Above the unread pages of a book.

They are fifteen or so. When I was thus,
I huddled in school coats, my satchel hung
Lop-sided on my shoulder. Without fuss
These enter adolescence; being young

Seems good to them, a state we cannot reach,
No talk of 'awkward ages' now. I see
How childish gazes staring out of each
Unfinished face prove me incredibly

Old-fashioned. Yet at least I have the chance
To size up several stages – young yet old,
Doing the twist, mocking an 'old-time' dance:
So many ways to be unsure or bold.

My Grandmother

She kept an antique shop – or it kept her.
Among Apostle spoons and Bristol glass,
The faded silks, the heavy furniture,
She watched her own reflection in the brass
Salvers and silver bowls, as if to prove
Polish was all, there was no need of love.

And I remember how I once refused
To go out with her, since I was afraid.
It was perhaps a wish not to be used
Like antique objects. Though she never said
That she was hurt, I still could feel the guilt
Of that refusal, guessing how she felt.

Later, too frail to keep a shop, she put
All her best things in one long, narrow room.
The place smelt old, of things too long kept shut,
The smell of absences where shadows come
That can't be polished. There was nothing then
To give her own reflection back again.

And when she died I felt no grief at all,
Only the guilt of what I once refused.
I walked into her room among the tall
Sideboards and cupboards – things she never used
But needed: and no finger-marks were there,
Only the new dust falling through the air.

The Diamond Cutter

Not what the light will do but how he shapes it
And what particular colours it will bear,

And something of the climber's concentration
Seeing the white peak, setting the right foot there.

Not how the sun was plausible at morning
Nor how it was distributed at noon,

And not how much the single stone could show
But rather how much brilliance it would shun;

Simply a paring down, a cleaving to
One object, as the star-gazer who sees

One single comet polished by its fall
Rather than countless, untouched galaxies.

Old Woman

So much she caused she cannot now account for
As she stands watching day return, the cool
Walls of the house moving towards the sun.
She puts some flowers in a vase and thinks
  'There is not much I can arrange
In here and now, but flowers are suppliant

As children never were. And love is now
A flicker of memory, my body is
My own entirely. When I lie at night
I gather nothing now into my arms,
  No child or man, and where I live
Is what remains when men and children go.'

Yet she owns more than residues of lives
That she has marked and altered. See how she
Warns time from too much touching her possessions
By keeping flowers fed, by polishing
  Her fine old silver. Gratefully
She sees her own glance printed on grandchildren.

Drawing the curtains back and opening windows
Every morning now, she feels her years
Grow less and less. Time puts no burden on
Her now she does not need to measure it.
  It is acceptance she arranges
And her own life she places in the vase.

A Disabled Countryman

You acknowledge change but not without grief.
You are long-sighted, point the chalk horse out
Reined in on the horizon,
And you approve the cows in the middle-distance,
A jar, close by,
Of wall-flowers is a blur, but you with pleasure
Smell it, smile, and go silent.

Only a moment, though, only a moment.
You are off on the crops, niceties of description,
Forecasts of meteorologists and, most,
The book of biology swiftly turned in your mind,
Page after page lit with your intuitions.

You are a man who is stranger to regret
As the sun down-going does not grieve though it sheds
Its blood on the ritual sky.
It does not grieve but welcomes the moon taking over
With its court of attendant stars.
So you, a countryman who is now disabled
Must watch what once you used to do. You never
Envy the active ones.
The present is your province since it's wide
Enough to let the future enter it.

And the past is part of that open book whose pages
Have room for notes. Nothing is static for you.
You say a snowdrop has always been your favourite
Flower. That fits. You have its gentleness
Concealing toughness, and a suffering
Which goes with the land, the seasons and the weather.
You take on pain as birds take buffets from
The wind, then gather strength and fly and fly.

Mirrors

Was it a mirror then across a room,
A crowded room of parties where the smoke
Rose to the ceiling with the talk? The glass
Stared back at me a half-familiar face
Yet something hoped for. When at last you came
It was as if the distant mirror spoke.

That loving ended as all self-love ends
And teaches us that only fair-grounds have
The right to show us halls of mirrors where
In every place we look to see our stare
Taunting our own identities. But love
Perceives without a mirror in the hands.

A Game of Cards

Determined to be peaceful, we played cards,
Dealt out the hands and hid from one another
Our power. Our only words were weightless words
Like 'Your turn', 'Thank you' – words to soothe and smother;
Our pulses, slowed to softness, moved together.

So we became opponents and could stare
Like strangers, guessing what the other held.
There was no look of love or passion there.
The pasteboard figures sheltered us, compelled
Each one to win. Love was another world.

And yet within the concentration which
Held us so fast, some tenderness slipped in,
Some subtle feeling which could deftly breach
The kings and queens and prove the pasteboard thin:
Another battle thundered to begin.

ELIZABETH JENNINGS

San Paolo Fuori le Mura, Rome

It is the stone makes stillness here. I think
There could not be so much of silence if
The columns were not set there rank on rank,
For silence needs a shape in which to sink
And stillness needs these shadows for its life.

My darkness throws so little space before
My body where it stands, and yet my mind
Needs the large echoing churches and the roar
Of streets outside its own calm place to find
Where the soft doves of peace withdraw, withdraw.

The alabaster windows here permit
Only suggestions of the sun to slide
Into the church and make a glow in it;
The battering daylight leaps at large outside
Though what slips here through jewels seems most fit.

And here one might in his discovered calm
Feel the great building draw away from him,
His head bent closely down upon his arm,
With all the sun subsiding to a dim
Past-dreamt-of peace, a kind of coming home.

For me the senses still have their full sway
Even where prayer comes quicker than an act.
I cannot quite forget the blazing day,
The alabaster windows or the way
The light refuses to be called abstract.

Skies

Never the same for a second;
In the South, ecstatic blue
Until a brief dark cloud
Sends down huge hail-stones,
Then the blue returns.

In the North, skies are more subtle,
Clouds more curiously shaped
And always changeable –
Like sheep, like balloons, like puffs of smoke.
Except for the sea,

Skies are the most eye-drawing things,
Especially at night when
Moon can be severally-shaped,
Stars glitter and we have named them,
We should find names for our skies.

Meteorologists have listed the clouds
But, as far as I know, no-one
Has found worthy names for the whites,
The daring blue, the darkness.
Soon, perhaps, somebody will

But it will have to be a poet.

Song for the Swifts

The swifts have now returned.
They volley, parry, play with the new light,
Dance under pieces of cloud then, out of sight,
Tease us with the pleasure of their flight,
Become our luxury too. The wind's weight
Is once again to be learned,

To be taught to us by each swift.
Melancholies are carried away in the stride
Of the tamed clouds and spring has opened wide
Its windows, these birds assisting. They have defied
Drowning waves, peaks few men have tried
And they have come to lift

Our minds and natures too.
Envy cowers with so much to be shared,
Love revives as we count up the paired,
Unthinkingly mating birds. Cold winds are repaired
By South the swifts have brought and we are snared
By joy, know what to do.

However dark our lands,
Wisdom is in our bloodstream not in brain
Alone and we take instinct on again
Watching these birds and the soon-to-bear-fruit grain,
And what we never thought we could attain
Falls, the uneaten apple, in our hands.

PHILIP LARKIN

Philip Larkin is one of the most famous and skilful poets writing today. Moreover he has written about events or reactions that he shares with the majority of people in his own times, so his main interest is in the humanity of the people whom he sees around him, even though he often writes about them from the point of view of an outsider who watches their social activities without actually joining in.

Larkin was born in 1922 in Coventry, where his father was City Treasurer. He was educated at King Henry VIII School, Coventry, and at St John's College, Oxford, where he became friends with his fellow student, Kingsley Amis, who later wrote *Lucky Jim* and other witty novels. Owing to his poor eyesight, Larkin was declared unfit for military service, so in 1943 he obtained a job as a librarian in Shropshire. He took the techniques of librarianship very seriously and won a series of promotions which led to his becoming University Librarian at Hull in 1956.

As an unknown young man he wrote two novels. In *Jill* he drew a perceptive portrait of the student from a working-class background who just did not fit in with university life, and in *A Girl in Winter* he made considerable use of his experiences as a librarian in a provincial town. *Jill* was published by the Fortune Press and attracted little notice, but *A Girl in Winter*, under Faber's imprint, received prestigious reviews. Today they are both in print and give sharp, arresting impressions of life during the austerity of the post-war years.

In 1945 Larkin published a volume of poetry called *The North Ship*, which has subsequently been recognised for its real worth. Despite the slow start of his early books, Larkin still went on resolutely trying to improve his poetic skills in a new vein that was natural and direct. Some excellent poems by him were published in literary magazines but at first they were too different from the fashionable poetry of the early 1950s to win attention. In 1955 a small publishing firm, the Marvell Press, bravely risked publishing a volume of these poems called *The*

Less Deceived. Soon the poems in this collection were receiving serious attention from the poetry-reading public, and Robert Conquest included several of them in his important anthology *New Lines* (1956), which championed a new, less opaque approach to writing poetry.

Larkin has continued to write just a few poems each year. His practice has been to publish them first in magazines and then to collect them together, as in *The Whitsun Weddings* (1964) and *High Windows* (1974). The first of these volumes won the Queen's Gold Medal for Poetry. Larkin's poetry continued to reach a very high standard and to maintain the virtues that had been shown in his previous collection. A minority of his later poems have used new techniques and treated new subjects, but most of them would not have seemed out of place if they had been included in *The Less Deceived*. This has led some critics to complain that he has shown little development as a poet.

Meanwhile, he has continued to be involved with other types of writing and editing. For instance, in 1970 he published *All What Jazz*, having been jazz correspondent of the *Daily Telegraph* for several years; and in 1973 he edited *The Oxford Book of Twentieth Century Verse*.

As Larkin developed a distinctive style of his own in writing poetry, he came to disagree more and more with the view of T. S. Eliot (1888–1965) that 'Poets in our civilisation, as it exists at present, must be difficult.' He was encouraged in this direction by his reading of the poetry of Hardy and Betjeman. He has gratefully praised Betjeman for believing 'that a poem's meaning should be communicated directly and not by symbol', for writing 'comprehensible poems in a regular metre' and for feeling so fascinated by the variety of personality that is shown by men and women. Similarly Larkin has explained in a radio talk that: 'When I came to Hardy it was with the sense of relief that I didn't have to try and jack myself up to a concept of poetry that lay outside my own life.' Hardy gave Larkin the confidence to write directly and honestly about his own feelings and about people whom he imagined, such as the narrators of many of his poems, who are usually not Larkin himself even if they resemble him in some respects – such as being single. Consequently Hardy and Betjeman helped him to invent a new style of poetry which is easy to understand yet is obviously modern in its subject matter. This has led him to say on the radio that 'a poet has to enjoy writing poetry, and the reader enjoy reading it, or they are both wasting their time'.

One of the methods that he has used very successfully is to tell a story and to create a dramatic situation as part of it. He throws a person rather like himself into this situation, and lets the poem develop out of this personal context. For instance, in *The Whitsun Weddings* (included in *Nine Modern Poets*) the narrator tells of one afternoon about twenty-five years ago when many honeymoon couples were travelling by train to London, and then on to some seaside place such as Torquay (today their counterparts might fly to Spain or Majorca). The narrator is travelling to London too, and soon he becomes aware of the repeated scene on each station platform, as the wedding guests see the bridal couples on to the train and say goodbye to them by hurling confetti and smutty advice. This repeated pattern of events stirs emotions in the poet and his final comment is an optimistic one, feeling that the bridal couples are creating a new future in several senses of the phrase:

> 'And as the tightening brakes took hold, there swelled
> A sense of falling, like an arrow-shower
> Sent out of sight, somewhere becoming rain.'

As often happens, Larkin ends by evaluating the event or experience that he has described. The details that he includes show that he is taking a close and sympathetic interest in the lives of the ordinary people who share his train journey. The novelist and poet John Wain has described this achievement very clearly in an article in *Critical Quarterly*:

> 'Larkin stands back and looks. But to look, for an artist of his receptivity, is to feel ... such contemplation – rapt, unwavering, emphatic – is a way of "joining in", and the only way that art knows. The poet contrasts the essentially self-preoccupied mood of the young couples with his own sense of involvement in a moment of complicated multiple experience. ... In a sense the poet's involvement is greater than theirs; he sees and understands just what it is that each

participant feels, and then puts them together to form one complete experience.'

An equally typical poem, written some years later, is *Show Saturday*. Larkin chooses what is a familiar event in modern life. He describes it as a novelist would and chooses practical details that help us to envisage the scene; for instance, he notices that the prize leeks look like church candles because they have been washed so very white, and that each exhibitor has laid out six beans with one split open to reveal the inside of the bean. He takes a genuine interest in the people who go to the show, from the husbands who are 'watchful as weasels' to their 'car-tuning curt-haired sons'. Larkin tells us almost nothing about the part that he played in the show or the motive that took him to it; he is merely a modest but alert and vigilant observer. However, he ends by recognising how strongly the participants feel that the show is an indispensable part of the yearly round of events, and an essential stimulant of community feeling. He suggests that the many details that he enumerates coalesce into some strength of local feeling which all the visitors and participants share, and so he implies his approval of what the show achieves by ending with a fine conservative hope. 'Let it always be there.'

PHILIP LARKIN

To the Sea

To step over the low wall that divides
Road from concrete walk above the shore
Brings sharply back something known long before –
The miniature gaiety of seasides.
Everything crowds under the low horizon:
Steep beach, blue water, towels, red bathing caps,
The small hushed waves' repeated fresh collapse
Up the warm yellow sand, and further off
A white steamer stuck in the afternoon –

Still going on, all of it, still going on!
To lie, eat, sleep in hearing of the surf
(Ears to transistors, that sound tame enough
Under the sky), or gently up and down
Lead the uncertain children, frilled in white
And grasping at enormous air, or wheel
The rigid old along for them to feel
A final summer, plainly still occurs
As half an annual pleasure, half a rite,

As when, happy at being on my own,
I searched the sand for Famous Cricketers,
Or, farther back, my parents, listeners
To the same seaside quack, first became known.
Strange to it now, I watch the cloudless scene:
The same clear water over smoothed pebbles,
The distant bathers' weak protesting trebles
Down at its edge, and then the cheap cigars,
The chocolate-papers, tea-leaves, and, between

The rocks, the rusting soup-tins, till the first
Few families start the trek back to the cars.
The white steamer has gone. Like breathed-on glass
The sunlight has turned milky. If the worst
Of flawless weather is our falling short,
It may be that through habit these do best,
Coming to water clumsily undressed
Yearly; teaching their children by a sort
Of clowning; helping the old, too, as they ought.

Show Saturday

Grey day for the Show, but cars jam the narrow lanes.
Inside, on the field, judging has started: dogs
(Set their legs back, hold out their tails) and ponies (manes
Repeatedly smoothed, to calm heads); over there, sheep
(Cheviot and Blackface); by the hedge, squealing logs
(Chain Saw Competition). Each has its own keen crowd.
In the main arena, more judges meet by a jeep:
The jumping's on next. Announcements, splutteringly loud,

Clash with the quack of a man with pound notes round his hat
And a lit-up board. There's more than just animals:
Bead-stalls, balloon-men, a Bank, a beer-marquee that
Half-screens a canvas Gents; a tent selling tweed,
And another, jackets. Folks sit about on bales
Like great straw dice. For each scene is linked by spaces
Not given to anything much, where kids scrap, freed,
While their owners stare different ways with incurious faces.

The wrestling starts, late; a wide ring of people; then cars;
Then trees; then pale sky. Two young men in acrobats' tights
And embroidered trunks hug each other; rock over the grass,
Stiff-legged, in a two-man scrum. One falls: they shake hands.
Two more start, one grey-haired: he wins, though. They're not so much fights
As long immobile straining that end in unbalance
With one on his back, unharmed, while the other stands
Smoothing his hair. But there are other talents –

The long high tent of growing and making, wired-off
Wood tables past which crowds shuffle, eyeing the scrubbed spaced
Extrusions of earth: blanch leeks like church candles, six pods of
Broad beans (one split open), dark shining-leafed cabbages – rows
Of single supreme versions, followed (on laced
Paper mats) by dairy and kitchen; four brown eggs, four white eggs,

Four plain scones, four dropped scones, pure excellences that
enclose
A recession of skills. And, after them, lambing-sticks, rugs,

Needlework, knitted caps, baskets, all worthy, all well done,
But less than the honeycombs. Outside, the jumping's over.
The young ones thunder their ponies in competition
Twice round the ring; then trick races, Musical Stalls,
Sliding off, riding bareback, the ponies dragged to and fro for
Bewildering requirements, not minding. But now, in the
background,
Like shifting scenery, horse-boxes move; each crawls
Towards the stock entrance, tilting and swaying, bound

For far-off farms. The pound-note man decamps.
The car park has thinned. They're loading jumps on a truck.
Back now to private addresses, gates and lamps
In high stone one-street villages, empty at dusk,
And side roads of small towns (sports finals stuck
In front doors, allotments reaching down to the railway);
Back now to autumn, leaving the ended husk
Of summer that brought them here for Show Saturday –

The men with hunters, dog-breeding wool-defined women,
Children all saddle-swank, mugfaced middle-aged wives
Glaring at jellies, husbands on leave from the garden
Watchful as weasels, car-tuning curt-haired sons –
Back now, all of them, to their local lives:
To names on vans, and business calendars
Hung up in kitchens; back to loud occasions
In the Corn Exchange, to market days in bars,

To winter coming, as the dismantled Show
Itself dies back into the area of work.
Let it stay hidden there like strength, below
Sale-bills and swindling; something people do,
Not noticing how time's rolling smithy-smoke
Shadows much greater gestures; something they share
That breaks ancestrally each year into
Regenerate union. Let it always be there.

Here

Swerving east, from rich industrial shadows
And traffic all night north; swerving through fields
Too thin and thistled to be called meadows,
And now and then a harsh-named halt, that shields
Workmen at dawn; swerving to solitude
Of skies and scarecrows, haystacks, hares and pheasants,
And the widening river's slow presence,
The piled gold clouds, the shining gull-marked mud,

Gathers to the surprise of a large town:
Here domes and statues, spires and cranes cluster
Beside grain-scattered streets, barge-crowded water,
And residents from raw estates, brought down
The dead straight miles by stealing flat-faced trolleys,
Push through plate-glass swing doors to their desires –
Cheap suits, red kitchen-ware, sharp shoes, iced lollies,
Electric mixers, toasters, washers, driers –

A cut-price crowd, urban yet simple, dwelling
Where only salesmen and relations come
Within a terminate and fishy-smelling
Pastoral of ships up streets, the slave museum,
Tattoo-shops, consulates, grim head-scarfed wives;
And out beyond its mortgaged half-built edges
Fast-shadowed wheat-fields, running high as hedges,
Isolate villages, where removed lives

Loneliness clarifies. Here silence stands
Like heat. Here leaves unnoticed thicken,
Hidden weeds flower, neglected waters quicken,
Luminously-peopled air ascends;
And past the poppies bluish neutral distance
Ends the land suddenly beyond a beach
Of shapes and shingle. Here is unfenced existence:
Facing the sun, untalkative, out of reach.

PHILIP LARKIN

Going, Going

I thought it would last my time –
The sense that, beyond the town,
There would always be fields and farms,
Where the village louts could climb
Such trees as were not cut down;
I knew there'd be false alarms

In the papers about old streets
And split-level shopping, but some
Have always been left so far;
And when the old part retreats
As the bleak high-risers come
We can always escape in the car.

Things are tougher than we are, just
As earth will always respond
However we mess it about;
Chuck filth in the sea, if you must:
The tides will be clean beyond.
– But what do I feel now? Doubt?

Or age, simply? The crowd
Is young in the M1 cafe;
Their kids are screaming for more –
More houses, more parking allowed,
More caravan sites, more pay.
On the Business Page, a score

Of spectacled grins approve
Some takeover bid that entails
Five per cent profit (and ten
Per cent more in the estuaries): move
Your works to the unspoilt dales
(Grey area grants)! And when

You try to get near the sea
In summer . . .
                                        It seems, just now,
To be happening so very fast;
Despite all the land left free
For the first time I feel somehow
That it isn't going to last,

That before I snuff it, the whole
Boiling will be bricked in
Except for the tourist parts –
First slum of Europe: a role
It won't be so hard to win,
With a cast of crooks and tarts.

And that will be England gone,
The shadows, the meadows, the lanes,
The guildhalls, the carved choirs.
There'll be books; it will linger on
In galleries; but all that remains
For us will be concrete and tyres.

Most things are never meant.
This won't be, more likely: but greeds
And garbage are too thick-strewn
To be swept up now, or invent
Excuses that make them all needs.
I just think it will happen, soon.

MCMXIV

Those long uneven lines
Standing as patiently
As if they were stretched outside
The Oval or Villa Park,
The crowns of hats, the sun
On moustached archaic faces
Grinning as if it were all
An August Bank Holiday lark;

And the shut shops, the bleached
Established names on the sunblinds,
The farthings and sovereigns,
And dark-clothed children at play
Called after kings and queens,
The tin advertisements
For cocoa and twist, and the pubs
Wide open all day;

And the countryside not caring:
The place-names all hazed over
With flowering grasses, and fields
Shadowing Domesday lines
Under wheat's restless silence;
The differently-dressed servants
With tiny rooms in huge houses,
The dust behind limousines;

Never such innocence,
Never before or since,
As changed itself to past
Without a word – the men
Leaving the gardens tidy,
The thousands of marriages
Lasting a little while longer:
Never such innocence again.

Homage to a Government

Next year we are to bring the soldiers home
For lack of money, and it is all right.
Places they guarded, or kept orderly,
Must guard themselves, and keep themselves orderly.
We want the money for ourselves at home
Instead of working. And this is all right.

It's hard to say who wanted it to happen,
But now it's been decided nobody minds.
The places are a long way off, not here,
Which is all right, and from what we hear
The soldiers there only made trouble happen.
Next year we shall be easier in our minds.

Next year we shall be living in a country
That brought its soldiers home for lack of money.
The statues will be standing in the same
Tree-muffled squares, and look nearly the same.
Our children will not know it's a different country.
All we can hope to leave them now is money.

The Explosion

On the day of the explosion
Shadows pointed towards the pithead:
In the sun the slagheap slept.

Down the lane came men in pitboots
Coughing oath-edged talk and pipe-smoke,
Shouldering off the freshened silence.

One chased after rabbits; lost them;
Came back with a nest of lark's eggs;
Showed them; lodged them in the grasses.

So they passed in beards and moleskins,
Fathers, brothers, nicknames, laughter,
Through the tall gates standing open.

At noon, there came a tremor; cows
Stopped chewing for a second; sun,
Scarfed as in a heat-haze, dimmed.

The dead go on before us, they
Are sitting in God's house in comfort,
We shall see them face to face –

Plain as lettering in the chapels
It was said, and for a second
Wives saw men of the explosion

Larger than in life they managed –
Gold as on a coin, or walking
Somehow from the sun towards them,

One showing the eggs unbroken.

Reference Back

That was a pretty one, I heard you call
From the unsatisfactory hall
To the unsatisfactory room where I
Played record after record, idly,
Wasting my time at home, that you
Looked so much forward to.

Oliver's *Riverside Blues*, it was. And now
I shall, I suppose, always remember how
The flock of notes those antique negroes blew
Out of Chicago air into
A huge remembering pre-electric horn

The year after I was born
Three decades later made this sudden bridge
From your unsatisfactory age
To my unsatisfactory prime.

Truly, though our element is time,
We are not suited to the long perspectives
Open at each instant of our lives.
They link us to our losses: worse,
They show us what we have as it once was,
Blindingly undiminished, just as though
By acting differently we could have kept it so.

No Road

Since we agreed to let the road between us
Fall to disuse,
And bricked our gates up, planted trees to screen us,
And turned all time's eroding agents loose,
Silence, and space, and strangers – our neglect
Has not had much effect.

Leaves drift unswept, perhaps; grass creeps unmown;
No other change.
So clear it stands, so little overgrown,
Walking that way tonight would not seem strange,
And still would be allowed. A little longer,
And time will be the stronger.

Drafting a world where no such road will run
From you to me;
To watch that world come up like a cold sun,
Rewarding others, is my liberty.
Not to prevent it is my will's fulfilment.
Willing it, my ailment.

PHILIP LARKIN

Self's the Man

Oh, no one can deny
That Arnold is less selfish than I.
He married a woman to stop her getting away
Now she's there all day,

And the money he gets for wasting his life on work
She takes as her perk
To pay for the kiddies' clobber and the drier
And the electric fire,

And when he finishes supper
Planning to have a read at the evening paper
It's *Put a screw in this wall* –
He has no time at all,

With the nippers to wheel round the houses
And the hall to paint in his old trousers
And that letter to her mother
Saying *Won't you come for the summer*.

To compare his life and mine
Makes me feel a swine:
Oh, no one can deny
That Arnold is less selfish than I.

But wait, not so fast:
Is there such a contrast?
He was out for his own ends
Not just pleasing his friends;

And if it was such a mistake
He still did it for his own sake,
Playing his own game.
So he and I are the same,

Only I'm a better hand
At knowing what I can stand
Without them sending a van –
Or I suppose I can.

EDWIN MORGAN

Edwin Morgan was born in 1920 and has spent most of his life in the city of Glasgow. As he describes it: 'I was born in Glasgow and have lived in and around the city most of my life. I identify strongly with it as a place and would be reluctant to live anywhere else. My father worked as a clerk with a local firm of iron and steel scrap merchants and eventually became a director of the firm. Both he and my mother were hard-working, conscientious, anxious persons, with a strong sense of what is ordered and right.'

As a boy Morgan inherited from his Scottish parents the Puritan idea that working hard was an important virtue. He was a studious, earnest boy who went to church and Sunday school, learnt large parts of the Bible by heart, and won a scholarship from Rutherglen Academy to Glasgow High School. He finally took an honours degree at Glasgow University in 1947 and stayed on to become a lecturer in English and later a professor, but his studies at the university were interrupted by five years in the army, during which he was sent, via the long voyage round the Cape of Good Hope, to Egypt, Palestine and Lebanon. The people of the Middle East made a deep impression on him, but service in the army had a deadening effect on his creative abilities, so he did not publish his first volume of poetry until he was thirty-two, and he wrote his best poetry after he was forty. His experiences aboard a troopship on this long voyage round the Cape became a major topic in one of his longer poems, *The Cape of Good Hope*, and they also provide a moment of exaltation in *The Unspoken* when the soldiers crowd on to the decks of the troopship to see the full moon rising above the so-called Horn of Africa, the cape that forms its north-eastern tip.

Between the ages of thirty-two and sixty-two Morgan continually published volumes of poetry and won a wide variety of medals and Arts Council awards. In 1969 he was included with Edward Brathwaite and Alan Bold in *Penguin Modern Poets 15*. In 1982 he published his collected *Poems of Thirty Years*.

One obvious point that must be made about Morgan is that

he is an essentially Scottish poet. 'If you are a Scot,' he has said, 'you are a Scot and you have certain problems that come with the territory.' Although he has written highly imaginative poetry that is concerned with time and space in the style of science fiction, he also concentrates in a distinctive body of his poems on producing realistic portrayals of scenes and people in Scotland, especially Glasgow. The girls in *Linoleum Chocolate* are running with their two rolls of linoleum down London Road, Glasgow; the pair of lovers in *Strawberries* sit eating strawberries on a hot afternoon as the summer lightning is beginning to light up the Kilpatrick Hills, just north-west of Glasgow; in *Trio* the three happy young people, laughing under the Christmas lights, are carrying their purchases along Buchanan Street in Glasgow, and the tiny dog wears a Royal Stewart tartan coat.

Morgan's Glasgow Sonnets introduce contrast into his presentation of the city by painting a grimmer picture – of Glasgow slum houses beginning to fall to bits as the last inhabitants depart. These sonnets are like Sassoon's poems about World War I: they make an intelligent and humane comment on a situation that is really unbearable. In a variety of other poems he gives us convincing, if often brief, glimpses of Glasgow with 'The roofs and cranes and the dark rain'. These poems show us Glasgow as it really is with the cranes and Victorian church-spires and the high-rise flats competing for places on the skyline as the hulls of new ships rise above the crumbling tenements. Even *The Unspoken*, which begins with the full moon rising over Africa, ends with the more familiar topic of 'Glasgow days and grey weathers when the rain beat on the bus shelter'.

As well as being fascinated by the appearance of Glasgow, Morgan is also intrigued by the colloquial language spoken by its inhabitants. He shows this in his sympathetic portrait of the drunk who gets on the bus on Good Friday. He also reveals his deep interest in a different way by translating other poets' work into Scots dialect (for instance, one of his translations from a Russian poet begins: 'I'm no a dab at fleechin wi douce words'), and he has even translated speeches from Shakespeare's *Macbeth*.

For these reasons Morgan must be included among the poets who have written at least some of their poetry in *Lallans*, which is the word that Burns applied to the natural language of the

Lowland Scots. In the area that lies roughly between Glasgow and Edinburgh, the original Celtic population who spoke Gaelic were driven out between AD 500 and 1000 by Germanic peoples very similar to the Anglo-Saxons who invaded England. They spoke a language whose grammar was very similar to that of English, but was enriched by the addition of many concrete and forceful words used by the Scottish peasants. This was used as the natural language for poetry by some medieval poets such as Dunbar, some eighteenth-century poets such as Burns, and some twentieth-century poets such as Hugh MacDiarmid, Goodsir Smith, and of course Morgan himself.

Here is part of a speech by Lady Macbeth, translated into modern Scots by Edwin Morgan:

> Cwa starnless nicht,
> rowed i the smeek and reek of daurkest hell,
> that my ain eident knife gang blindly in,
> and heaven keekna through the skuggy thack
> to cry 'Haud back!'

Shakespeare's original version is in *Macbeth* Act I, Scene 5, and begins, 'Come, thick night . . .'.

It is in character for Morgan to say that 'My own main interest as a poet is bound to centre in Scotland'. Moreover, some of his readers apply to Scotland, or even just to Glasgow, the lines that he addresses to a woman in one of his comparatively early poems:

> 'If only we'd been strangers
> we'd been floating off to Timor,
> we'd be shimmering on the Trades
> in a blue jersey boat
> with shandies, flying fish,
> a pace of dolphins
> to the copra ports.'

Nevertheless, there are two different claims that we might make for Morgan as a poet. One claim, still associated with his poems about Glasgow, would be his success at conveying sudden snapshot scenes of city life, with directness and simplicity. For instance, *Linoleum Chocolate* gives us an amusing, instantaneous glimpse of the two girls 'running laughing' down the main road, while a man picks up the bar of chocolate that one of them has dropped and helps them to bite it while they continue giggling; in *Trio* Morgan, in similar vein, catches the Christmas hilarity of the crowd, despite the onset of a frosty winter evening.

These poems illustrate what Morgan himself has expressed in the following words: 'I just suddenly discovered that I *could* write about simple things happening in Glasgow to me or to other people.' In most of the poems that he wrote in this manner he is in an optimistic mood and he gives the impression that the people he is describing are enjoying themselves. He is like a photographer who has been lucky to take a photograph at just the right moment. In some ways it is a pity that he did not keep the label *Instamatic* for these poems, but he had already applied it to the poems in which he reconstructed fifty-two gruesome incidents that he had taken from the newspapers. His best poems imply that the people he describes have suddenly found a thrilling moment of happiness and success; though Morgan does not spoil the moment by commenting too much about it or becoming too solemn and earnest, he includes just enough detail to be convincing.

It is, however, possible to make larger claims for Morgan than this. One can argue that he has been of major importance as a versatile and experimental pioneer, in testing new forms of poetry. Three examples of Morgan's experimentation with new forms are his space fiction, political poetry, and concrete poetry. They are all very much mediums of the moment and represent a general optimism in Morgan's mind about the ability of human beings to adapt to the demands of modern times. Morgan takes space exploration seriously, so when he describes in *The Unspoken* how excited he was to hear that the Russians had launched a second satellite with a dog on board, he is being sincere. In his poems *In Sobieski's Shield* and *From the Domain of Arnheim* he has studied the problems that human beings would experience in being removed from earth and rehoused on some distant star:

'We moved on down, arm in arm.
I know you would have thought it was a dream,
but we were there. And those were trumpets –
tremendous round the rocks –
while they were burning fires of trash and mammoth's
  bones.'

As for making politics a topic in poetry, Morgan seems to have tried this only occasionally, such as in the poem where he thinks about the death of Ché Guevara, the revolutionary who helped Castro to gain control of Cuba and later died in an unsuccessful attempt to invade Fascist Bolivia; or in *Starryveldt*, which uses games with words to express his indignation about the régime that imposed the policy of apartheid on South Africa. Morgan regards these experiments as fundamentally very serious. He has said: 'I am interested in the kind of poetry which British poets seem to find difficult to write. You might roughly describe it as political. It is a poetry which is really aware of the poet and artist being a citizen with a place in society and duties and responsibilities in society. My poet is a man who looks at his society and feels that he has something to say about it.'

The violence associated with twentieth-century politics is one of Morgan's particular preoccupations, as shown in the poems about King Billy, a gang-leader in pre-war Glasgow. Similarly, he has experimented enthusiastically with concrete poetry, in which the visual arrangement of the poem contributes to its meaning. Critics who fail to appreciate Morgan's experimental poems at least give him this much credit: 'He is very much a performer, and when he fails it is through an excess of virtuosity.' In other words, Morgan's critics believe that he has put too much exertion into experimental writing, when the newness of the technique demands sustained effort and a considerable originality from the poet. But Morgan's natural skill has been to describe straightforward, happy scenes from Glasgow life in a realistic, apparently artless way. His best poetry is also his simplest and by its nature it leaves the critics little to say about it except for obvious praise.

EDWIN MORGAN

An Addition to the Family: for *M.L.*

A musical poet, collector of basset-horns,
was buttering his toast down in Dumbartonshire
when suddenly from behind the breakfast newspaper
the shining blade stopped scraping
and he cried to his wife, 'Joyce, listen to this! –
"Two basset-hounds for sale, house-trained, keen hunters" –
Oh we must have them! What d'you think?' 'But dear,
did you say *hounds*?' 'Yes yes, hounds, hounds –'
'But Maurice, it's *horns* we want, you must be over
in the livestock column, what would we do
with a basset-hound, you can't play a hound!'
'It's Beverley it says, the kennels are at Beverley –'
'But Maurice –' '– I'll get some petrol, we'll be there by
lunchtime –'
'But a dog, two dogs, where'll we put them?'
'I've often wondered what these dogs are like –'
'You mean you don't even –' 'Is there no more marmalade?'
'– don't know what they look like? And how are we to feed
them?
Yes, there's the pot dear.' 'This stuff's all peel, isn't it?'
'Well, we're at the end of it. But look, these two great –'
'You used to make marmalade once upon a time.'
'They've got ears down to here, and they're far too –'
'Is that half past eight? I'll get the car out.
See if I left my cheque-book on the –' 'Maurice,
are you mad? What about your horns?' 'What horns,
what are you talking about? Look Joyce dear,
if it's not on the dresser it's in my other jacket.
I believe they're wonderful for rabbits –'
So the musical poet took his car to Beverley
with his wife and his cheque-book, and came back home
with his wife and his cheque-book and two new hostages
to the unexpectedness of fortune.
The creatures scampered through the grass, the children
came out with cries of joy, there seemed to be nothing
dead or dying in all that landscape.

Fortune bless the unexpected cries!
Life gathers to the point of wishing it,
a mocking pearl of many ventures. The house
rolled on its back and kicked its legs in the air.
And later, wondering farmers as they passed would hear
behind the lighted window in the autumn evening
two handsome mellow-bosomed basset-hounds
howling to a melodious basset-horn.

The Old Man and the Sea

And a white mist rolled out of the Pacific
and crept over the sand, stirring nothing –
cold, cold as nothing is cold
on those living highways, moved in
over the early morning trucks,
chilling the drivers in their cabins
(one stops for a paper cup
of coffee, stares out through the steam
at the mist, his hands on the warm cup
imagine the coldness, he throws out the cup
and swears as the fog rolls in, drives on
frowning to feel its touch on his face) –
and seagulls came to shriek at cockcrow
swooping through the wakening farms,
and the smoke struggled from the lumber camps
up into the smoke from the sea,
hovered in the sunless morning
as a lumberman whistled at the pump,
and sea-mist took the flash from the axe.
And above the still lakes of Oregon
and the Blue Mountains into Idaho
eastward, white wings brushing the forests,
a white finger probing the canyon
by Wood River, delicate, persistent, at last
finding by the half-light, in a house of stone,
a white-bearded man like an old sea-captain
cleaning a gun. – Keep back the sea,

keep back the sea! No reassurance
in that daybreak with no sun,
his blood thin, flesh patched and scarred,
eyes grown weary of hunting
and the great game all uncaught.
It was too late to fight the sea.
The raised barrel hardly gleamed
in that American valley, the shot
insulted the morning, crude and quick
with the end of a great writer's life –
fumbling nothing, but leaving questions
that echo beyond Spain and Africa.
Questions, not answers, chill the heart here,
a chained dog whining in the straw,
the gunsmoke marrying the sea-mist,
and silence of the inhuman valleys.

The Unspoken

When the troopship was pitching round the Cape
In '41, and there was a lull in the night uproar of seas and winds, and a sudden full moon
swung huge out of the darkness like the world it is,
and we all crowded onto the wet deck, leaning on the rail, our arms on each other's shoulders, gazing at the savage outcrop of great Africa,
and Tommy Cosh started singing 'Mandalay' and we joined in with our raucous chorus of the unforgettable song,
and the dawn came up like thunder like that moon drawing the water of our yearning
though we were going to war, and left us exalted,
that was happiness,
but it is not like that.

When the television newscaster said
the second sputnik was up, not empty
but with a small dog on board,

a half-ton treasury of life orbiting a thousand miles above the
thin television masts and mists of November,
in clear space, heard, observed,
the faint far heartbeat sending back its message
steady and delicate,
and I was stirred by a deep confusion of feelings,
got up, stood with my back to the wall and my palms pressed
hard against it, my arms held wide
as if I could spring from this earth –
not loath myself to go out that very day where Laika had shown
man,
felt my cheeks burning with old Promethean warmth
rekindled – ready –
covered my face with my hands, seeing only an animal
strapped in a doomed capsule, but the future
was still there, cool and whole like the moon,
waiting to be taken, smiling even
as the dog's bones and the elaborate casket of aluminium
glow white and fuse in the arc of re-entry,
and I knew what I felt was history,
its thrilling brilliance came down,
came down,
comes down on us all, bringing pride and pity,
but it is not like that.

But Glasgow days and grey weathers, when the rain
beat on the bus shelter and you leaned slightly against me, and
the back of your hand touched my hand in the shadows, and
nothing was said,
when your hair grazed mine accidentally as we talked in a café,
yet not quite accidentally,
when I stole a glance at your face as we stood in a doorway and
found I was afraid
of what might happen if I should never see it again,
when we met, and met, in spite of such differences in our lives,
and did the common things that in our feeling
became extraordinary, so that our first kiss
was like the winter morning moon, and as you shifted in my
arms

it was the sea changing the shingle that changes it
as if for ever (but we are bound by nothing, but like smoke
to mist or light in water we move, and mix) –
O then it was a story as old as war or man,
and although we have not said it we know it,
and although we have not claimed it we do it,
and although we have not vowed it we keep it,
without a name to the end.

Strawberries

There were never strawberries
like the ones we had
that sultry afternoon
sitting on the step
of the open french window
facing each other
your knees held in mine
the blue plates in our laps
the strawberries glistening
in the hot sunlight
we dipped them in sugar
looking at each other
not hurrying the feast
for one to come
the empty plates
laid on the stone together
with the two forks crossed
and I bent towards you
sweet in that air
in my arms
abandoned like a child
from your eager mouth
the taste of strawberries
in my memory
lean back again
let me love you

let the sun beat
on our forgetfulness
one hour of all
the heat intense
and summer lightning
on the Kilpatrick hills

let the storm wash the plates

Linoleum Chocolate

Two girls running,
running laughing,
laughing lugging
two rolls of linoleum
along London Road –
a bar of chocolate
flies from the pocket
of the second, and a man
picks it up for her, she takes it
and is about to pocket it
but then unwraps it
and the girls have a bite
to recruit the strength
of their giggling progress.

Trio

Coming up Buchanan Street, quickly, on a sharp winter evening
a young man and two girls, under the Christmas lights –
The young man carries a new guitar in his arms,
the girl on the inside carries a very young baby,
and the girl on the outside carries a chihuahua.
And the three of them are laughing, their breath rises
in a cloud of happiness, and as they pass
the boy says, 'Wait till he sees this but!'
The chihuahua has a tiny Royal Stewart tartan coat like a teapot-
holder,
the baby in its white shawl is all bright eyes and mouth like
favours in a fresh sweet cake,
the guitar swells out under its milky plastic cover, tied at the
neck with silver tinsel tape and a brisk sprig of mistletoe.
Orphean sprig! Melting baby! Warm chihuahua!
The vale of tears is powerless before you.
Whether Christ is born, or is not born, you
put paid to fate, it abdicates
under the Christmas lights.
Monsters of the year
go blank, are scattered back,
can't bear this march of three.

– And the three have passed, vanished in the crowd
(yet not vanished, for in their arms they wind
the life of men and beasts, and music,
laughter ringing them round like a guard)
at the end of this winter's day.

Glasgow Sonnet

A mean wind wanders through the backcourt trash.
Hackles on puddles rise, old mattresses
puff briefly and subside. Play-fortresses
of brick and bric-à-brac spill out some ash.
Four storeys have no windows left to smash,
but in the fifth a chipped sill buttresses
mother and daughter, the last mistresses
of that black block condemned to stand, not crash.
Around them the cracks deepen, the rats crawl.
The kettle whimpers on a crazy hob.
Roses of mould grow from ceiling to wall.
The man lies late since he has lost his job.
Smokes on one elbow, letting his coughs fall thinly into an air
too poor to rob.

Good Friday

Three o'clock. The bus lurches
round into the sun. 'D's this go –'
he flops beside me – 'right along Bath Street?
– Oh tha's, tha's all right, see I've
got to get some Easter eggs for the kiddies.
I've had a wee drink, ye understand –
ye'll maybe think it's a – funny day
to be celebrating – well, no, but ye see
I wasny working, and I like to celebrate
when I'm no working – I don't say it's right
I'm no saying it's right, ye understand – ye understand?
But anyway tha's the way I look at it –
I'm no boring you, eh? – ye see today,
take today, I don't know what today's in aid of,
whether Christ was – crucified or was he –
rose fae the dead like, see what I mean?
You're an educatit man, you can tell me –
– Aye, well. There ye are. It's been seen
time and again, the working man

has nae education, he jist canny – jist
hasny got it, know what I mean,
he's jist bliddy ignorant – Christ aye,
bliddy ignorant. Well –' The bus brakes violently,
he lunges for the stair, swings down – off,
into the sun for his Easter eggs,
on very
  nearly
    steady legs.

Aberdeen Train

Rubbing a glistening circle
on the steamed-up window I framed
a pheasant in a field of mist.
The sun was a great red thing somewhere low,
struggling with the milky scene. In the furrows
a piece of glass winked into life,
hypnotized the silly dandy; we
hooted past him with his head cocked,
contemplating a bottle-end.
And this was the last of October,
a Chinese moment in the Mearns.

Ché

Even after the body
had been roughly brought
down to Vallegrande
from the hills, and the eyes
had that meaningless glaze
staring at no world,
eyes took meaning from
his slightly parted lips
showing the teeth
in a smile – no rage,

no throes, nothing
but that uncanny pro-
jection of consciousness
and a dead man putting
fate in bondage
to him. Bolivia:
what other bondages
will shiver in the cane-break
even in steel, and will break,
uniforms and proclamations
ploughed under by the very grass
itself – it rises
into the voices of forests.
For the dead wander
among its deep roots
like water, and push
the green land into heroes.
They grow in understanding,
tree, tree, man, man,
move like shadows.
Blossoms brushed
by silent bandoliers
spring out in shock and
back into place.
But jungles break.
Down from the mountains
miles and miles
a marble face,
a broken body.
The marble is only
broken by a smile.

Starryveldt

starryveldt
   slave
southvenus
   serve
SHARPEVILLE
   shove
shriekvolley
   swerve
shootvillage
   save
spoorvengeance
   stave
spadevoice
   starve
strikevault
   strive
subvert
   starve
smashverwoerd
   strive
scattervoortrekker
   starve
spadevow
   strive
sunvast
   starve
survive
   strive
SO: VAEVICTIS

NORMAN NICHOLSON

Norman Nicholson is an exceptionally 'local' poet. He has lived almost all his life in one town, and that was where his parents too had lived almost all their lives. He was born in 1914 in Millom, a small town on the northern shore of the estuary of the river Duddon, in a remote south-western corner of Cumbria. Most of Nicholson's poetry and prose describes his native town, its working-class characters, and the beauty of the Lakeland scenery that is so close at hand.

Millom has proved a classic example of a town that relied too heavily on one method of earning a living. The ironworks which for years dominated the town finally closed in 1968, resulting in much hardship for the local inhabitants. Certainly west Cumberland has endured more than its fair share of unemployment and poverty during Nicholson's lifetime. Nicholson never protests against this in the manner of a propagandist, but he tells the plain truth about his home town and the struggles of its people whom he has known so well. Consequently he is able to voice the feelings and speech of the working class very directly.

A typical example of the Cumbrian working class was his grandmother, who loved him but found him a puzzling namby-pamby, and accused him of being unable to say boo to a goose. In writing about his grandmother and other members of his family he draws a vivid picture of the distinctive personalities of the people who lived in Millom.

The old iron mines and smelting works (growing fewer and fewer), plus a few new factories that have tried to create a future for the area, have left untouched the occasional streaks of beauty that still defy destruction. The Duddon can no longer boast of being a river 'remote from industry' as it was in Wordsworth's lifetime, but Nicholson delights in the unusual visual effects that are created by the odd juxtaposition of mine and castle or factories and salt-marshes beside the shallow arms of the sea.

Of course, a small town quickly changes its appearance once its main industry has gone, and present-day Millom does not altogether resemble the town as it was described by Nicholson in the 1940s or even the 1950s. Today, the modest Victorian streets which Nicholson described are still there, and still make up a distinct part of the town – between the railway station and the remains of the ironworks. These working-class streets, built in straight lines at right angles to one another, have a geometric appearance that is unusual in England. Market Street's houses retain their decorative facing of khaki-coloured stones which hide the fact that below the surface they are made of the same local slate as houses in the neighbouring streets. Consequently this street still looks a little superior to the others, just as Nicholson describes it in one of his poems. However, the only remaining traces of the old ironworks are diminishing heaps of grey slag and the former offices, once pretentious in a solemn, Victorian way, but now partly abandoned and dilapidated and partly rebuilt in inferior materials.

Not far from the site of the old ironworks, there are plenty of signs of new activities and successful adaptations. For instance, a well-known shoe-making firm has opened a very new-looking factory, while the old port of Haverigg has been modernised and redecorated so that it can act as a fashionable little harbour for the yachts of the wealthy. Yet the whole area retains one of the major characteristics that Nicholson stresses in his poetry: it is all hemmed in by a circle of high hills whose steep sides turn towards Millom. Snow still survives unmelted on parts of these abrupt hillsides even in April. And of course the River Duddon still flows slowly towards the sea within this circle of surrounding hills. A few miles inland it creeps through marshes which the high tides of the equinoxes reach only twice a year, but finally it penetrates the wide levels of flat sand to reach the choppy waters of the Irish Sea.

To describe this scene as he knew it a few years ago, and to bring to life the personalities of his relatives and neighbours, Nicholson has developed a manner of writing that is honest, direct and hard-hitting. In describing his neighbours in their small town, jammed between precarious factories and intrusive seas, Nicholson has developed his own style and his own voice. He sounds completely contemporary, yet he retains some of the traditional use of rhyme and metre that we associate with English poetry of past ages.

But Nicholson's most succesful achievement is that he writes clearly yet originally; it is characteristic of him that he praises Wordsworth the man in a style that never imitates Wordsworth the poet.

Nicholson excels as a painter of landscapes in verse; moreover he describes the familiar sights that are right on his doorstep, rather than the beauty spots a few miles away that the tourist usually sees. Nicholson shows us Whitehaven, where the houses on the eastern hillsides and the pit-heads on the sea-shore throw the town into shadow. He pictures the 'damp autumnal sunlight' that only half illuminates the chimneys, rubble-tips and castle-crowned ridge of the neighbouring town of Egremont. Most of all, he brings to life the many moods of weather that give variety and character to Millom – from the iron slag drifting in the November wind to the summer flies dancing in the 'jittery' sunshine. He manages to include in his descriptions of his home town the intense emotional relationships between members of the families and the distinctive images of the different seasons. So in writing about Millom he is writing about the essentials of human life.

NORMAN NICHOLSON

Have You Been to London?

'Have you been to London?'
My grandmother asked me.
'No.' –
China dogs on the mantelshelf,
Paper blinds at the window,
Three generations simmering on the bright black lead,
And a kettle filled to the neb,
Spilled over long ago.

I blew into the room, threw
My scholarship cap on the rack;
Wafted visitors up the flue
With the draught of my coming in –
Ready for Saturday's mint imperials,
Ready to read
The serial in *Titbits*, the evangelical
Tale in the parish magazine,
Under the green
Glare of the gas,
Under the stare of my grandmother's Queen.

My grandmother burnished her sleek steel hair –
Not a tooth in her jaw,
Nor alphabet in her head,
Her spectacles lost before I was born,
Her lame leg stiff in the sofa corner,
Her wooden crutch at the steady:
'They shut doors after them
In London,' she said.

I crossed the hearth and thumped the door *to*;
Then turned to Saturday's stint,
My virtuosity of print
And grandmother's wonder:
Reading of throttler and curate,
Blood, hallelujahs and thunder,
While the generations boiled down to one
And the kettle burned dry
In a soon grandmotherless room;

Reading for forty years,
Till the print swirled out like a down-catch of soot
And the wind howled round
A world left cold and draughty,
Un-latched, un-done,
By all the little literate boys
Who hadn't been to London.

Boo to a Goose

'You couldn't say *Boo* to a goose', my grandmother said
When I skittered howling in from the back street – my head
With a bump the size of a conker from a stick that someone
  threw,
Or my eyes rubbed red
From fists stuffed in to plug the blubbing. 'Not *Boo* to a goose,'
  she said,
But coddled me into the kitchen, gave me bread
Spread with brown sugar – her forehead,
Beneath a slashed, ash-grey bark of hair,
Puckered in puzzle at this old-fashioned child
Bright enough at eight to read the ears off
His five unlettered uncles, yet afraid
Of every giggling breeze that blew.
'There's nowt to be scared about,' she said,
'A big lad like you!'

But not as big as a goose –
                  or not the geese I knew,
Free-walkers of Slagbank Green.
From morning-lesson bell to supper-time
They claimed lop-sided common-rights between
Tag-ends of sawn-off, two-up-two-down streets
And the creeping screes of slag.
They plucked their acres clean
Of all but barley-grass and mud. Domesticated but never tamed,
They peeked down on you from their high
Spiked periscopes. No dog would sniff within a hundred yards
Of their wing-menaced ground.

At the first sound
Of a bicycle ring they'd tighten ranks,
Necks angled like bayonets, throttles sizzling,
And skein for the bare knees and the cranking shanks.
They were guarded like Crown Jewels. If any man were seen
To point a finger to a feather
He'd end up with boot-leather for his dinner.
They harried girls in dreams – and my lean
Spinning-wheel legs were whittled even thinner
From trundling round the green's extremest hem
To keep wide of their way.
No use daring me to say
Boo to them.

The girls grew up and the streets fell down;
Gravel and green went under the slag; the town
Was eroded into the past. But half a century later
Three geese – two wild, streaked brown-grey-brown
As the bog-cottoned peat, and one white farm-yard fly-off –
Held sentry astride a Shetland lochan. The crumbled granite
Tumbled down brae and voe-side to the tide's
Constricted entry; the red-throated diver jerked its clown-
striped neck, ducked, disappeared and perked up from the water
A fly-cast further on. The three geese took no notice.
But the moment I stepped from the hide of the car
The white one stiffened, swivelled, lowered its trajectory,
And threatened towards me. Then,
Under the outer arctic's summer arc of blue,
With a quick blink that blacked out fifty years
And a forgotten fear repeating in my stomach,
I found myself staring, level-along and through,
The eyes of that same slagbank braggart
I couldn't say *Boo* to.

NORMAN NICHOLSON

The Black Guillemot

Midway between Fleswick and St Bees North Head,
The sun in the west,
All Galloway adrift on the horizon;
The sandstone red
As dogwood; sea-pink, sea campion and the sea itself
Flowering in clefts of the cliff –
And down on one shelf,
Dozen on dozen pressed side by side together,
White breast by breast,
Beaks to the rock and tails to the fish-stocked sea,
The guillemots rest

Restlessly. Now and then,
One shifts, clicks free of the cliff,
Wings whirling like an electric fan –
Silhouette dark from above, with under-belly gleaming
White as it banks at the turn –
Dives, scoops, skims the water,
Then, with all Cumberland to go at, homes
To the packed slum again,
The rock iced with droppings.

I swing my binoculars into the veer of the wind,
Sight, now, fifty yards from shore,
That rarer auk: all black,
But for two white patches where the wings join the back,
Alone like an off-course migrant
(Not a bird of his kind
Nesting to the south of him in England),
Yet self-subsistent as an Eskimo,
Taking the huff if so much as a feather
Lets on his pool and blow-hole
In the floating pack-ice of gulls.

But, turn the page of the weather,
Let the moon haul up the tides and the pressure-hose of spray
Swill down the lighthouse lantern – then,
When boats keep warm in harbour and bird-watchers in bed,

When the tumble-home of the North Head's rusty hull
Takes the full heave of the storm,
The hundred white and the one black flock
Back to the same rock.

Cleator Moor

From one shaft at Cleator Moor
They mined for coal and iron ore.
This harvest below ground could show
Black and red currants on one tree.

In furnaces they burnt the coal,
The ore was smelted into steel,
And railway lines from end to end
Corseted the bulging land.

Pylons sprouted on the fells,
Stakes were driven in like nails,
And the ploughed fields of Devonshire
Were sliced with the steel of Cleator Moor.

The land waxed fat and greedy too,
It would not share the fruits it grew,
And coal and ore, as sloe and plum,
Lay black and red for jamming time.

The pylons rusted on the fells,
The gutters leaked beside the walls,
And women searched the ebb-tide tracks
For knobs of coal or broken sticks.

But now the pits are wick with men,
Digging as dogs dig for a bone:
For food and life *we* dig the earth –
In Cleator Moor they dig for death.

Every wagon of cold coal
Is fire to drive a turbine wheel;
Every knuckle of soft ore
A bullet in a soldier's ear.

The miner at the rockface stands,
With his segged and bleeding hands
Heaps on his head the fiery coal,
And feels the iron in his soul.

Egremont

November sunlight floats and falls
Like soapsuds on the castle walls.
Where broken groins are slanted west
The bubbles touch the stone and burst,
And the moist shadows dribble down
And slime the sandy red with brown.

Here the hawkweed still contrives
Sustenance for mouse-ear leaves;
On fallen lintels groundsel rubs
Its heads of seed like lather-blobs;
And ragwort's stubborn flowers hold
Trayfuls of their pinchbeck gold.

Rain erases the written stone.
Boss and dog-tooth now are gone;
But yet the sandstone vaults and walls
Are scutcheoned with heraldic tales,
Of when Scots crossed the Roman fosse
And foraged down from Solway Moss.

Still the moated dungeons hide
Legends of poverty and pride,
And murdered skulls are stuffed with lore
Of pillage, plunder, famine, fear,
And dirk has carved upon the bone:
'Blood will not show on the red stone'.

The damp autumnal sunlight drips
On chimneys, pit-shafts, rubble-tips.
Centuries of feudal weight
Have made men stoop towards their feet.
They climb no rocks nor stare around,
But dig their castles in the ground.

Castles in the red ore made
Are buttressed, tunnelled, turreted,
And like a moat turned inside out
The pit-heaps trap the sieging light;
With lantern-flints the miners spark
And gouge their windows to the dark.

Here in the hollows the men store,
Rich as rubies, the red ore;
And rock and bones are broken both
When the stone spine is theft from earth.
The crime defiles like a red mud
The ore, the sandstone, and the blood.

But the robbed earth will claim its own
And break the mines and castles down
When Gabriel from heaven sent
Blows the Horn of Egremont,
Tabulates the tenants' needs
And reassumes the title-deeds.

On the Closing of Millom Ironworks

September 1968

Wandering by the heave of the town park, wondering
Which way the day will drift,
On the spur of a habit I turn to the feathered
Weathercock of the furnace chimneys.
But no grey smoke-tail

Pointers the mood of the wind. The hum
And blare that for a hundred years
Drummed at the town's deaf ears
Now fills the air with the roar of its silence.
They'll need no more to swill the slag-dust off the windows;
The curtains will be cleaner
And the grass plots greener
Round the Old Folk's council flats. The tanged autumnal mist
Is filtered free of soot and sulphur,
And the wind blows in untainted.
It's beautiful to breathe the sharp night air.
But, morning after morning, there
They stand, by the churchyard gate,
Hands in pockets, shoulders to the slag,
The men whose fathers stood there back in '28,
When their sons were at school with me.
The town
Rolls round the century's bleak orbit.
Down
On the ebb-tide sands, the five-funnelled
Battleship of the furnace lies beached and rusting;
Run aground, not foundered;
Not a crack in her hull;
Lacking but a loan to float her off.
The Market
Square is busy as the men file by
To sign on at the 'Brew'. But not a face
Tilts upward, no-one enquires of the sky.
The smoke prognosticates no how
Or why of any practical tomorrow.
For what does it matter if it rains all day?
And what's the good of knowing
Which way the wind is blowing
When whichever way it blows it's a cold wind now?

To the River Duddon

I wonder, Duddon, if you still remember
An oldish man with a nose like a pony's nose,
Broad bones, legs long and lean but strong enough
To carry him over Hard Knott at seventy years of age.
He came to you first as a boy with a fishing-rod
And a hunk of Ann Tyson's bread and cheese in his pocket,
Walking from Hawkshead across Walna Scar;
Then a middle-aged Rydal landlord,
With a doting sister and a government sinecure,
Who left his verses gummed to your rocks like lichen,
The dry and yellow edges of a once-green spring.
He made a guide-book for you, from your source
There where you bubble through the moss on Wrynose
(Among the ribs of bald and bony fells
With screes scratched in the turf like grey scabs),
And twist and slither under humpbacked bridges –
Built like a child's house from odds and ends
Of stones that lie about the mountain side –
Past Cockley Beck Farm and on to Birk's Bridge,
Where the rocks stride about like legs in armour,
And the steel birches buckle and bounce in the wind
With a crinkle of silver foil in the crisp of the leaves;
On then to Seathwaite, where like a steam-navvy
You shovel and slash your way through the gorge
By Wallabarrow Crag, broader now
From becks that flow out of black upland tarns
Or ooze through golden saxifrage and the roots of rowans;
Next Ulpha, where a stone dropped from the bridge
Swims like a tadpole down thirty feet of water
Between steep skirting-boards of rock; and thence
You dribble into lower Dunnerdale
Through wet woods and wood-soil and woodland flowers,
Tutson, the St John's-wort with a single yellow bead,
Marsh marigold, creeping jenny and daffodils;
Here from hazel islands in the late spring
The catkins fall and ride along the stream
Like little yellow weasels, and the soil is loosed
From bulbs of the white lily that smells of garlic,

And dippers rock up and down on rubber legs,
And long-tailed tits are flung through the air like darts;
By Foxfield now you taste the salt in your mouth,
And thrift mingles with the turf, and the heron stands
Watching the wagtails. Wordsworth wrote:
'Remote from every taint of sordid industry.'
But you and I know better, Duddon.
For I, who've lived for nearly thirty years
Upon your shore, have seen the slagbanks slant
Like screes into the sand, and watched the tide
Purple with ore back up the muddy gullies,
And wiped the winter dust from the farmyard damsons.
A hundred years of floods and rain and wind
Have washed your rocks clear of his words again,
Many of them half-forgotten, brimming the Irish Sea,
But that which Wordsworth knew, even the old man
When poetry had failed like desire, was something
I have yet to learn, and you, Duddon,
Have learned and re-learned to forget and forget again.
Not the radical, the poet and heretic,
To whom the water-forces shouted and the fells
Were like a blackboard for the scrawls of God,
But the old man, inarticulate and humble,
Knew that eternity flows in a mountain beck –
The long cord of the water, the shepherd's numerals
That run upstream, through the singing decades of dialect.
He knew, beneath mutation of year and season,
Flood and drought, frost and fire and thunder,
The blossom on the rowan and the reddening of the berries,
There stands the base and root of the living rock,
Thirty thousand feet of solid Cumberland.

On Duddon Marsh

This is the shore, the line dividing
The dry land from the waters, Europe
From the Atlantic; this is the mark
That God laid down on the third day.
Twice a year the high tide sliding,
Unwrapping like a roll of oil-cloth, reaches
The curb of the mud, leaving a dark
Swipe of grease, a scaled-out hay
Of wrack and grass and gutterweed. Then
For full three hundred tides the bare
Turf is unwatered except for rain:
Blown wool is dry as baccy; tins
Glint in the sedge with not a sight of man
For two miles round to drop them there.
But once in spring and once again
In autumn, here's where the sea begins.

St Luke's Summer

The low sun leans across the slanting field,
And every blade of grass is striped with shine
And casts its shadow on the blade behind,
And dandelion clocks are held
Like small balloons of light above the ground.

Beside the trellis of the bowling green
The poppy shakes its pepper-box of seed;
Groundsel feathers flutter down;
Roses exhausted by the thrust of summer
Lose grip and fall; the wire is twined with weed.

The soul, too, has its brown October days –
The fancy run to seed and dry as stone,
Rags and wisps of words blown through the mind;
And yet, while dead leaves clog the eyes,
Never-predicted poetry is sown.

NORMAN NICHOLSON

To the Memory of a Millom Musician

Harry Pelleymounter,
Day by half-pay day,
Served saucepans, fire-lighters, linseed oil
Over his father's counter;
But hard on shutting-up time
He snapped the yale and stayed
Alone with the rolled linoleum
And made the shop-dusk twang.

Harry played
Saxophone, piano,
Piano-accordion
At Christmas party and Saturday hop,
While we in the after-homework dark
Rang smut-bells, sang
'Yes, yes, YES, we have no',
And clocked ink-smitted fingers
At a down-at-heel decade.

The crumbling 'Thirties
Were fumbled and riddled away;
Dirty ten bob coupons
Dropped from the pockets of war.
And Harry, dumped in the lateral
Moraine of middle-age,
Strummed back the golden dole-days
When the boys with never a chance
Went without dinner
For a tanner for the dance.

Now Harry's daughter,
Fatherless at fifteen,
Is knitting a history thesis
Of Millom in between
Her youth and Harry's: –
Statistics of gas and water
Rates, percentage of unemployed,

Standard of health enjoyed
By the bare-foot children the police ran dances
To buy boots for – and Harry played.

Pulling at threads of the dead years,
The minutes taken as read –
Spectacled, earnest, unaware
That what the Chairman left unsaid,
The print in the dried-up throat, the true
Breath of the paper bones, once blew
Through Harry's soft-hummed, tumbled tunes
She never listened to.

Old Man at a Cricket Match

'It's mending worse,' he said,
Bending west his head,
Strands of anxiety ravelled like old rope,
Skitter of rain on the scorer's shed
His only hope.

Seven down for forty-five,
Catches like stings from a hive,
And every man on the boundary appealing –
An evening when it's bad to be alive,
And the swifts squealing.

Yet without boo or curse
He waits leg-break or hearse,
Obedient in each to law and letter –
Life and the weather mending worse,
Or worsening better.

Bond Street

'Bond Street,' I said, 'Now where the devil's that?' –
The name of one whose face has been forgotten. –
He watched me from a proud-as-Preston hat;
His briefcase fat with business. 'See, it's written
First on my list. Don't you know your own town?' –
'Bond Street?' – Turning it over like an old coin,
Thumbing it, testing for signs. – 'I copied it down
From a map in the Reading Room. In the mean-
time, I've a policy here . . .' – Yes, on a *map*
Bond Street once looked the first of streets, more
Rakish than the Prince of Wales, the peak of the cap
Jaunted at then ungathered orchards of ore,
Damsons of haematite. Yet not a house
Was built there and the road remained unmade,
For there was none to pay the rates – a mouse
And whippet thoroughfare, engineered in mud,
Flagged with the green-slab leaves of dock and plantain.
A free run for the milk cart to turn round
From either of the two back-alleys shunted
End-on against it. But the birds soon found
Sites where the Council couldn't. From last year's broccoli and old
Brass bedsteads joggled in to make a fence,
Among the pigeon lofts and hen-huts, in the cold
Green-as-a-goosegog twilight, the throstles sense
That here is the one street in all the town
That no-one ever died in, that never failed
Its name or promise. The iron dust blows brown.
I turned to my enquirer. – 'Bond Street I know well.
'You'll sell no insurance there.' – 'I could insure
The deaf and dumb,' he replied, 'against careless talk.' –
'Whatever you choose,' I said. 'A mile past the Square,
Then ask again. Hope you enjoy your walk.'

Whitehaven

In this town the dawn is late.
For suburbs like a waking beast
Hoist their backbones to the east,
And pitheads at the seaward gate
Build barricades against the light.
Deep as trenches streets are dug
Beneath entanglements of fog,
And dull and stupid the tide lies
Within the harbour's lobster claws.

Curlews wheel on the north wind,
Their bills still moist with Solway sand,
And eaves slide up from the wide bays
With rumours of the Hebrides.
But anchored to the jetty stones
Bladderwrack gnaws at the town's bones;
Barnacle, cockle, crab and mussel
Suck at the pier's decaying gristle;
And limpet keeps its tongue and dream
Reveted to an inch of home.
At the Atlantic's dying edge
The harbour now prepares for siege.
The mole intimidates the sea,
The bastions of the colliery
Are battlemented like a fort –
This is the last invasion port.

Not at Hastings, Medway, Skye,
But here on rock of Cumberland
Foreign invader last made stand.
In April 1778
Came John Paul Jones, the Yankee-Scot,
Apprentice from Kirkcudbrightshire,
Who learned his trade by box on ear,
Saw a wench whipped at Market Cross,
And spitting gold, without a toss
Of pence for publican or lover,
Sailed to the New World in a slaver.

He came at spring tide from the west.
The setting sun behind his mast;
His sails like gulls of flame that fell
On the scared ships behind the mole,
And scattered feathered fire on quays
And eighteenth-century warehouses.
Many a joiner's broken head
Paid for the knocks a 'prentice had,
And ashes of the harbour inns
Did penance for the landlord's sins.

This is the time that walls remember.
The lintels crack it with the street,
And pavements teach to passing feet,
And strangers feel within their veins
The cold suspicion of the stones.
Every man and woman born
In shade of this beleaguered town
Bargains brain and blood and thew
To keep the world from breaking through.

But the town's fort will fall at last
When the sea rams and bursts the mole,
And the mines vomit up their coal,
And dawn upon the breaking slate
Drops in an avalanche of light;
When Gabriel, the brigand, guides
His fiery frigate down the clouds,

Tears up the lighthouse in his hand
And waves it like a burning brand
Before the pennon, nailed to mast,
The Jolly Roger of the Blest –
Skull of Adam, Cross of Christ.
The merchants then will sell the town
To make their bartered souls their own,
Hoist high their white flag in the sky
And yield to heaven's piracy.

Innocents' Day

And Herod said: 'Sup-
posing you had been in my shoes, what would you have
Done different? – I was not thinking of myself. This
Child – whichever number might have come from the hat –
could
Scarcely have begun to make trouble for twenty or
Thirty years at least, and by that time
Ten to one I'd be dead and gone. What
Matters is to keep a straight succession none can
Argue about – someone acceptable to the occupying
Power, who nevertheless will enable us to pre-
serve our sense of being a nation,
Belonging and bound to one particular place.
I know my people. They are nomads, only
Squatters here as yet. They have never left the
Wilderness. Wherever in Asia Minor the grass
Seams a dune, or a well greens a wadi, or
Sheep can feed long enough for a tent to be pitched,
There they call home, praying for daily
Manna and a nightly pillar of fire. They are
Chronic exiles; their most-sung psalms look
Back to the time of looking back. They never see
Jerusalem in the here and now, but always long to
Be where they've never been that they may long to
Be where they really are.
If this child had
Lived, they'd have started the same blind trek, prospecting
In sand for their own footsteps, Yes,
Mothers are weeping in the streets of Judaea, but still the
Streets are there to weep in. If that child had lived,
Not a stone would have stayed on a stone, nor a brother with
brother,
Nor would all the Babylons of all the world
Have had water enough to swill away their tears.
That
I have put a stop to, at the price
Of a two-year crop of children, making
What future observers will undoubtedly judge a
Good bargain with history.

VERNON SCANNELL

Vernon Scannell was born in 1922 in Beeston, a suburb of Nottingham. His parents were members of the lower middle class who were often rather out of luck, but his father was rarely actually unemployed. As a boy Scannell lived in a variety of places, including Ireland, Beeston, Eccles (an industrial suburb of Manchester) and Aylesbury. He left school at fourteen without having a secondary education.

During his youth Scannell made considerable progress as an amateur boxer, and so boxing became one of his major interests. He later wrote:

> 'I have never subscribed to the commanding officer or headmaster view that "boxing makes a man of you", that it gives courage to the timid, bouncing self-confidence to the shy and changes the sneak and cad into an honest good sport. . . . But what it can do – and here it is like art – is give a man a chance to behave in a way that is beyond and above his normal capacity. . . . The good boxer, like the good artist, must have mastered all the basic orthodox techniques, but he must also be inventive and resourceful enough to adapt and modify these as new and unexpected problems are set before him.'

In his early years he was painfully torn apart by what seemed irreconcilable passions – boxing and writing. One part of him wanted to be a tough, fearless boxer, while the other wanted to be a romantic young writer like Byron or Rupert Brooke. 'It was a silly and unnecessary conflict,' he later wrote, 'but no less troubling for that, and it had its source, I think, in a kind of puritanical suspicion of the arts as something unmanly, emasculating.' But by the time he left the army he had escaped from this dilemma and had learnt to get pleasure from both boxing and literature.

Soon after the outbreak of World War II, Scannell thought it would be glamorous to enlist in a highland regiment, so he joined the Argyll and Sutherland Highlanders who transferred him to the Gordons. In his interesting autobiography, *The Tiger and the Rose*, he admits that 'I disliked the Army very much. I found that nothing in my temperament fitted me for the part of a soldier.' But he fought with the Gordon Highlanders in Montgomery's North African campaign and again in Normandy where he was wounded. Brought back to a hospital in England he found himself for the first time in his life actually possessing both the leisure and the eagerness to read novels and poetry. This stirred in him the long dormant ambition to be a writer.

In 1945 he decided that the only way to escape from the stultifying effect of army life was to desert. Consequently he lived with various bohemians in London and Leeds and earned money at a series of unskilled jobs such as selling flowers, making heads for dolls, shifting scenery in a theatre, selling perfume in markets and fighting as a professional boxer. In Leeds he was befriended by lecturers from the university's Department of English who allowed him to attend their lectures and to join the Boxing Club of the University Union; he won several university championships as a boxer at various weights. When he was arrested as a deserter in 1947, he was soon released on the grounds that a man who wanted to become a poet was obviously unfit psychologically to be a soldier.

Back in civilian life he found several jobs that were interesting but poorly paid, such as teaching in private schools. The oddness of these places can be judged by his description of one headmaster who was 'genial and kind-hearted with the appearance and manner of a failed music hall comedian and a touch of the not very successful con man'.

Later Scannell worked hard to achieve success as a poet and novelist. He also gave talks on the radio in the days before television became so popular. His adventurous, unusual life continued to convince him that 'under all the confusion, waste and perplexity of living, there has been a steady purpose, that, though I have often appeared to be, and believed myself to be, lost and blundering around in circles, I have in fact been moving fairly consistently in a particular direction, towards the fulfilment of my ambition to be a poet'.

One of the subjects that have fascinated him as a poet has been

World War I. When he was a boy the war photographs in the magazine *The Champion* provided him with:

> 'pictures of steel-helmeted men crouching below the sandbagged parapet of the trench, waiting to go over the top; pictures of shells exploding and throwing up huge black mushrooms of earth in the battered landscape of no-man's-land; pictures of gun-carriages, of stretcher-bearers struggling with their sad and patient burden through calf-deep mud, of tanks and broken churches . . . the shapes of unbearable terror, unbearable pain.'

Like Ted Hughes he also enjoyed listening to his father reminiscing about World War I; it brought home to him 'the landscapes, the sadness, the glory and the waste'. Consequently for Scannell himself 'the names of the great battles sounded and echoed in (his) skull like a roll of drums or distant gunfire'. This interest inspired later poems of his such as *August 1914* and *The Great War*, the second of which begins:

> 'Whenever war is spoken of
> I find
> The war that was called Great invades the mind.'

As for World War II in which he fought, he finds that he spent most of the periods when he was in action in a kind of trance, and so remembers only fragments of his experiences. But he remembers very vividly that: 'There can be nothing more emasculating, nothing more obscene and murderous than the pure physical terror that savages you when loud and violent death is screaming down from the sky and pounding the earth around you, smashing and pulping everything in its search for you.'

His memories of the war, which he describes in honest detail in his critical work *Not Without Glory* (1976), strengthened his rather unusual belief that the British poetry of World War II was as good as that of World War I, though it was very different.

Scannell's later autobiographical book, *A Proper Gentleman* (1977), recounts his very mixed experiences when he was awarded a writing fellowship on condition that he lived for nine months in the 'new village' of Berinsfield in Oxfordshire. Scannell found that Berinsfield proved in reality to be 'an unlettered jungle of red brick, bingo and booze', which reminded him of 'a large military depot or the married quarters of a prison, and the gaol-like aspect was increased by the huddle of roofs being overlooked by what I suppose was a water-tower but looked like the watch-tower of a prison-camp'.

This appointment, though exasperating in many ways, gave him the opportunity to read poetry in many schools, which he found an exhilarating experience because 'the only occasions when my pessimistic view of the poet's social or educative usefulness suffered revision was when I visited schools and found – as almost invariably I did find – an unself-conscious interest in and keen response to the poetry that I talked about and read to my audiences'.

Scannell's own poetry is fairly traditional. It shows the respect that he has always professed for the orthodox metres of English verse. It also reflects Scannell's own description of the themes that inspire him. He says his own writing has 'always been rooted in and fed by the life about me, my relationship with others, the loves, hates and irritations and delights of living with other people'. He has also enjoyed writing poetry that has given vivid accounts of his own experiences – such as his feelings when the spiced mists of an urban autumn blurred the suburbs of London, or his reactions when an Italian tenor began to sing with passion about romantic love.

In his work, Scannell chooses unusual, exciting words or combinations of words to describe human experiences that we have all shared or read about. He is often just a little witty and epigrammatic; he is never long-winded. His knack of selecting the pungent phrase prevents his poems from ever becoming ordinary. He is an inspired journalist who takes some typical incident of modern life and makes poetry out of it.

Picnic on the Lawn

Their dresses were splashed on the green
Like big petals; polished spoons shone
And tinkered with cup and saucer.
Three women sat there together.

They were young, but no longer girls.
Above them the soft green applause
Of leaves acknowledged their laughter.
Their voices moved at a saunter.

Small children were playing nearby;
A swing hung from an apple tree
And there was a sand pit for digging.
Two of the picknicking women

Were mothers. The third was not.
She had once had a husband, but
He had gone to play the lover
With a new lead in a different theatre.

One of the mothers said, 'Have you
Cherished a dream, a fantasy
You know is impossible; a childish
Longing to do something wildly

'Out of character? I'll tell you mine.
I would like to drive alone
In a powerful sports car, wearing
A headscarf and dark glasses, looking

'Sexy and mysterious and rich.'
The second mother smiled: 'I wish
I could ride through an autumn morning
On a chestnut mare, cool wind blowing

'The jet black hair I never had
Like smoke streaming from my head,
In summer swoop on a switchback sea
Surf-riding in a black bikini.'

She then turned to the childless one:
'And you? You're free to make dreams true.
You have no need of fantasies
Like us domestic prisoners.'

A pause, and then the answer came:
'I also have a hopeless dream:
Tea on the lawn in a sunny garden,
Listening to the voices of my children.'

Autumn

It is the football season once more
And the back pages of the Sunday papers
Again show the blurred anguish of goalkeepers.

In Maida Vale, Golders Green and Hampstead
Lamps ripen early in the surprising dusk;
They are furred like stale rinds with a fuzz of mist.

The pavements of Kensington are greasy;
The wind smells of burnt porridge in Bayswater,
And the leaves are mushed to silence in the gutter.

The big hotel like an anchored liner
Rides near the park; lit windows hammer the sky.
Like the slow swish of surf the tyres of taxis sigh.

On Ealing Broadway the cinema glows
Warm behind glass while mellow the church clock chimes
As the waiting girls stir in their delicate chains.

Their eyes are polished by the wind,
But the gleam is dumb, empty of joy or anger.
Though the lovers are long in coming the girls still linger.

We are nearing the end of the year.
Under the sombre sleeve the blood ticks faster
And in the dark ear of Autumn quick voices whisper.

It is time of year that's to my taste,
Full of spiced rumours, sharp and velutinous flavours,
Dim with the mist that softens the cruel surfaces,
Makes mirrors vague. It is the mist that I most favour.

VERNON SCANNELL

Here and Human

In the warm room, cushioned by comfort,
Idle at fireside, shawled in lamplight,
I know the cold winter night, but only
As a far intimation, like a memory
Of a dead distress whose ghost has grown genial.

The disc, glossy black as a conjurer's hat,
Revolves. Music is unwound: woodwind,
Strings, a tenor voice singing in a tongue
I do not comprehend or have need to –
'The instrument of egoism mastered by art' –

For what I listen to is unequivocal:
A distillation of romantic love,
Passion outsoaring speech. I understand
And, understanding, I rejoice in my condition:
This sweet accident of being here and human.

Later, as I lie in the dark, the echoes
Recede, the blind cat of sleep purrs close
But does not curl. Beyond the window
The hill is hunched under his grey cape
Like a watchman. I cannot hear his breathing.

Silence is a starless sky on the ceiling
Till shock slashes, stillness is gashed
By a dazzle of noise chilling the air
Like lightning. It is an animal screech.
Raucous, clawing: surely the language of terror.

But I misread it, deceived. It is the sound
Of passionate love, a vixen's mating call.
It lingers hurtful, a stink in the ear,
But soon it begins to fade. I breathe deep,
Feeling the startled fur settle and smooth. Then I sleep.

A Mystery at Euston

The train is still, releasing one loud sigh.
Doors swing and slam, porters importune.
The pigskin labelled luggage of the rich
Is piled on trolleys, rolled to waiting cars,
Grey citizens lug baggage to the place
Where fluttering kisses, craning welcomes wait.
A hoarse voice speaks from heaven, but not to her,
The girl whose luggage is a tartan grip
With broken zip, white face a tiny kite
Carried on the currents of the crowd.
The handsome stranger did not take her bag,
No talent-scout will ask her out to dine.
Her tights are laddered and her new shoes wince.
The Wimpy bar awaits, the single room,
The job as waitress, golden-knuckled ponce.
Whatever place she left – Glasgow, Leeds,
The village on the moors – there's no return.
Beyond the shelter of the station, rain
Veils the day and wavers at a gust,
Then settles to its absent-minded work
As if it has forgotten how to rest.

Schoolroom on a Wet Afternoon

The unrelated paragraphs of morning
Are forgotten now: the severed heads of kings
Rot by the misty Thames: the rose of York
And Lancaster are pressed between the leaves
Of history; negroes sleep in Africa.
The complexities of simple interest lurk
In inkwells and the brittle sticks of chalk:
Afternoon is come and English Grammar.

Rain falls as though the sky has been bereaved,
Stutters its inarticulate grief on glass
Of every lachrymose pane. The children read
Their books or make pretence of concentration,

Each bowed head seems bent in supplication
Or resignation to the fate that waits
In the unmapped forest of the future.
Is it their doomed innocence noon weeps for?

In each diminutive breast a human heart
Pumps out the necessary blood: desires,
Pains and ecstasies surfride each singing wave
Which breaks in darkness on the mental shores.
Each child is disciplined; absorbed and still
At his small desk. Yet lift the lid and see,
Amidst frayed books and pencils, other shapes:
Vicious rope, glaring blade, the gun cocked to kill.

A Kind of Hero

At school he was revered yet lonely.
No other boy, however much
He might dream of it,
Dared to be his friend.
He walked, gaunt and piratical,
All bones and grin,
Towards his inescapable end.

Revered, but not by authority,
He poured ink into the new hat
Of the French Master,
Painted the blackboard white,
Swore at the huge Principal,
Refused to bend
And invited him to a free fight.

In memory he is beautiful,
But only his desperate gold
Hair might have been so.
Vaguely we understood,
And were grateful, that he performed
Our lawless deeds:
Punished, he allowed us to be good.

The end: he was killed at Alamein.
He wore handcuffs on the troopship
Going out; his webbing
All scrubbed as white as rice;
And we, or others like us,
Were promoted
By his last, derisive sacrifice.

August 1914

The bronze sun blew a long and shimmering call
Over the waves of Brighton and Southend,
Over slapped and patted pyramids of sand,
Paper Union Jacks and cockle stalls;
A pierrot aimed his banjo at the gulls;
Small spades dug trenches to let the channel in
As nimble donkeys followed their huge heads
And charged. In the navy sky the loud white birds
Lolled on no wind, then, swinging breathless, skimmed
The somersaulting waves; a military band
Thumped and brayed, brass pump of sentiment;
And far from the beach, inland, lace curtains stirred,
A girl played Chopin while her sister pored
Over her careful sewing; faint green scent
Of grass was sharpened by a gleam of mint,
And, farther off, in London, horses pulled
Their rumbling drays and vans along the Strand
Or trundled down High Holborn and beyond
The Stadium Club, where, in the wounded world
Of five years later, Georges Carpentier felled
Bulldog Joe Becket in a single round.
And all is history; its pages smell
Faintly of camphor and dead pimpernel
Coffined in leaves, and something of the sand
And salt of holiday. But dead. The end
Of something never to be lived again.

VERNON SCANNELL

The Great War

Whenever war is spoken of
I find
The war that was called Great invades the mind:
The grey militia marches over land
A darker mood of grey
Where fractured tree-trunks stand
And shells, exploding, open sudden fans
Of smoke and earth.
Blind murders scythe
The deathscape where the iron brambles writhe;
The sky at night
Is honoured with rosettes of fire,
Flares that define the corpses on the wire
As terror ticks on wrists at zero hour.
These things I see,
But they are only part
Of what it is that slyly probes the heart:
Less vivid images and words excite
The sensuous memory
And, even as I write,
Fear and a kind of love collaborate
To call each simple conscript up
For quick inspection:
Trenches' parapets
Paunchy with sandbags; bandoliers, tin-hats.
Candles in dug-outs,
Duckboards, mud and rats.
Then, like patrols, tunes creep into the mind:
A long, long trail, *The Rose of No-Man's Land*,
Home Fire and *Tipperary*:
And through the misty keening of a band
Of Scottish pipes the proper names are heard
Like fateful commentary of distant guns:
Passchendaele, Bapaume, and Loos, and Mons.
And now,
Whenever the November sky
Quivers with a bugle's hoarse, sweet cry,

The reason darkens; in its evening gleam
Crosses and flares, tormented wire, grey earth
Splattered with crimson flowers,
And I remember,
Not the war I fought in
But the one called Great
Which ended in a sepia November
Four years before my birth.

Gunpowder Plot

For days these curious cardboard buds have lain
In brightly coloured boxes. Soon the night
Will come. We pray there'll be no sullen rain
To make these magic orchids flame less bright.

Now in the garden's darkness they begin
To flower: the frenzied whizz of Catherine-wheel
Puts forth its fiery petals and the thin
Rocket soars to burst upon the steel

Bulwark of a cloud. And then the guy,
Absurdly human phoenix, is again
Gulped by greedy flames: the harvest sky
Is flecked with threshed and glittering golden grain.

'Uncle! A cannon! Watch me as I light it!'
The women helter-skelter, squealing high,
Retreat; the paper fuse is quickly lit,
A cat-like hiss and spit of fire, a sly

Falter, then the air is shocked with blast.
The cannon bangs and in my nostrils drifts
A bitter scent that brings the lurking past
Lurching to my side. The present shifts,

Allows a ten-year memory to walk
Unhindered now; and so I'm forced to hear
The banshee howl of mortar and the talk
Of men who died; am forced to taste my fear.

I listen for a moment to the guns,
The torn earth's grunts, recalling how I prayed.
The past retreats. I hear a corpse's sons –
'Who's scared of bangers?' 'Uncle! John's afraid!'

End of a Season

The nights are drawing in; the daylight dies
With more dispatch each evening;
Traffic draws lit beads
Across the bridge's abacus.
Below, black waters jitter in a breeze.
The air is not yet cold
But woven in its woof of various blues,
Whiffs of petrol and cremated flowers,
A cunning thread runs through,
A thin premonitory chill.
The parks are closed. Lights beckon from the bars.
The sporting news has put on heavier dress.
It is not autumn yet
Though summer will not fill
Attentive hearts again with its warm yes.

Far from the city, too, the dark surprises:
Oak and sycamore hunch
Under their loads of leaves;
Plump apples fall; the night devises
Frail webs to vein the sleek skin of the plums.
The scent of stars is cold.
The wheel-ruts stumble in the lane, are dry and hard.
Night is a nest for the unhatched cries of owls;
As deep mines clench their gold
Night locks up autumn's voices in
The vaults of silence. Hedges are still shawled
With traveller's joy; yet windows of the inn
Rehearse a winter welcome.
Though tomorrow may be fine
Soon it will yield to night's swift drawing in.
The athletes of light evenings hibernate;
Their whites are folded round
Green stains; the night
Reminds with its old merchandise –
Those summer remnants on its highest boughs –
That our late dancing days
Are doomed if not already under ground.

The playground gates are chained; the swings hang still;
The lovers have come down
From their deciduous hill;
Others may climb again, but they will not.
And yet the heart resumes its weightier burden
With small reluctance; fares
Towards Fall, and then beyond
To winter with whom none can fool or bargain.

ANNE STEVENSON

Although Anne Stevenson was born in England and is married to an Englishman, and although she has lived, taught and published poetry in both England and Scotland, she is still fundamentally an American. Just as the subject of her poetry moves to and fro between the New World and Europe, so she herself has kept travelling. In 1970, for instance, she spent some time at the Radcliffe Institute for Independent Women at Harvard, before moving to Glasgow and subsequently to Dundee, where she was writing fellow for two years. She then went to Oxford to be a fellow of Lady Margaret Hall. In 1979 she moved to Hay on Wye in Wales, where she co-founded The Poetry Bookshop.

One of the most stable influences in her life was her father. As a child Anne thought of him chiefly as a pianist and she herself learnt to play the piano and the cello. When she was born in 1933 her father was actually studying philosophy in Cambridge, England. Later he became a lecturer in philosophy at several American universities, though he and his family often returned for holidays to the New England states of Vermont and Connecticut, of which they grew very fond, and which they thought of as two parts of the same home base.

She chose the University of Michigan as the place to study for her degree and it was as a student that she developed a deep emotional loyalty to the United States. For all these reasons Anne Stevenson has been very well placed to explain how the Americans regard both Britain and the British. In some of her descriptive poetry she explains how Britain appears to the American traveller as a 'cramped corner country' where 'severity is cherished'. But she holds a balance between noticing its countryside, with cornfields that 'lie naked in the burnt shires' after harvesting is over, and urban scenes where she sees 'wet roofs creeping for miles along wet bricks'.

At various times between 1960 and 1980 she held academic posts in Scotland, holding a post with the Open University in

Paisley and as Compton Fellow of Creative Writing at Dundee University. Consequently she has written several effective poems about visits with her children to various places on the Scottish coast, including Carnoustie and Boarhills on the east coast, north of Edinburgh, and Mallaig, a port on the west coast opposite the island of Skye.

At Carnoustie she notices what a 'northern look' the coast has; she comments on the absence of trees and the fact that the ocean looks 'serious'. Everywhere she notices the birds that glide like angels above these 'work-a-day' places.

In England she has held a number of temporary posts in universities and colleges, including the University of Durham and Lady Margaret Hall, Oxford. In recent years she has lived in Hay-on-Wye, where she was a partner in the running of a poetry bookshop. She grew very fond of this part of the country just to the west of the Welsh border, and also of the area that lies between Hay-on-Wye and the river Severn. Her choice of just the right details to describe this part of England and Wales reminds us tellingly of what it is like to walk, or even to drive, in this area. For instance, she notices:

> '. . . the westness of west here
> in England's last thatched, rivered
> county. Red ploughland. Green pasture.
> Black cattle. Quick water.'

Interestingly a guide book to this area emphasises exactly the same colours, saying that it 'is a land of reds and greens, the reds of the earth, the sandstone and the mountains, and the greens of the grass, the fertile crops and the hedgerow trees'.

In *Green Mountain, Black Mountain* she contrasts the woods of New England, still green in early autumn, with the Black Mountains just south of Hay-on-Wye, seen on a day in April when cold rain was falling on the half-melted snow. She wrote the poem as an elegy for her parents both of whom had recently died. Because she remembers her father so much more clearly as a musician than as an academic, she composed it as a sort of cantata that could easily be set to music. The final section of the poem imitates the various tunes of the British thrush and of the blackbird – which, she explains to her American readers, is 'low-voiced, melancholy, exquisite'. Another poem inspired by this same area on the Welsh border, but not included in this anthology, is called *Buzzard and Alder*; here she describes a buzzard landing on a bough of an alder tree with the effect that bird and tree become indistinguishable.

Anne Stevenson also has a talent for expressing the feminine (though not feminist) point of view. This is what the American poet Wallace Stevens was thinking of when he wrote: 'I am what is around me. Women understand this.' Anne Stevenson's brief poem *The Crush* is a candid, convincing expression of the feelings of a teenage girl who has fallen in love – more romantically than sensibly – for the first time. She cannot help looking at the young man who sits in the choir at church, and she cannot help walking past his house just to hear him play the piano, all the time ascribing to him the thrilling qualities that are possessed by the heroes of famous novels.

Other poems express the feminine point of view at a more mature age. When she takes her sons to paddle in pools of sea water at Boarhills, she regards them maternally as 'faces I have washed and scolded', and she notices that their voices 'return like footprints over the sandflats'. In *Poem to my Daughter* she expresses a mother's feelings towards her newly born daughter:

> '. . . nothing's more perfect
> than that bleating, razor-shaped cry
> that delivers a mother to her baby.
> The bloodcord snaps that held
> their sphere together. The child,
> tiny and alone, creates the mother.'

The poets who have influenced Anne Stevenson include several English writers of the period 1500–1660, such as Sir Thomas Wyatt, Sir Walter Raleigh, John Donne and Andrew Marvell, and also various twentieth-century Americans such as Robert Frost, Wallace Stevens and Elizabeth Bishop. Their work has encouraged her to develop a spare, economical and distinctive style that prunes away every unnecessary word. The quotation from *Poem to my Daughter* neatly illustrates this aspect of her style. 'Perfect' is really a very extreme word in its context and makes a very great claim for motherhood, but Anne

Stevenson makes no acknowledgment of how great are her claims, and does not complicate this one superlative by using any other word to qualify it. She leaves it to her reader to realise slowly exactly what she is saying. Similarly the word 'bleating' is a remarkable word in its context, but Anne Stevenson does not stop to qualify it by an apologetic phrase or a descriptive adverb. The word suggests that part of the relationship between a human mother and her daughter is merely like the animal relationship between a bleating lamb and a ewe. But the poem lets a single word say all this.

However, one rhetorical device that she permits herself is a characteristic type of repetition. For instance in *If I Could Paint Essences* she uses deliberate repetition in lines such as: 'A cloudness of clouds which are not like anything but clouds' and also: 'in such imaginings I lose sight of sight'. In the first stanza of *Swifts* she repeats not only the word 'little', but also the phrase 'The swifts are back':

> 'Spring comes little, a little. All April it rains.
> The new leaves stick in their fists. New ferns, still fiddleheads.
> But one day the swifts are back. Face to the sun like a child
> You shout, "The swifts are back!" '

So far we have looked at those poems in which Anne Stevenson speaks directly about her own feelings and tells us what she thinks or feels, for example when she sees the first swifts appear in spring or hears the first bleating cry of her newly-born daughter. But in another mood, she is *dramatic* in the sense that the Victorian poet Browning was dramatic, and she speaks not for herself but for characters she has imagined. Her most important contribution to dramatic poetry is a volume called *Correspondences* (1974), a family history in letters. In it she imagines past and present members of a New England family who write to each other between the years 1829 and 1972, revealing their emotional 'correspondences'. The letters describe the perplexing conflicts of the New England Puritan tradition. Some of the characters find it difficult to conform to the puritan ethic; some are caught up in paradoxical ideas of women's place in society; others lose their faith in an increasingly capitalistic vision of God. Themes of marriage and divorce, mother versus daughter, father versus son weave in and out of the narrative until, at the end, the structure of a whole way of life collapses with a series of nervous breakdowns, deaths, escapes and bewildered apologies. The heroine (who has many names, but is one character throughout) retreats at last to England, realising that 'nowhere is safe'.

'In the floodtide of Civitas Mundi
New England is dissolving like a green chemical.
Old England bleeds out to meet it in mid-ocean.
  Nowhere is safe.
It is a poem I can't continue.
It is American I can't contain . . .'

Besides her six volumes of poetry, Anne Stevenson has written a critical study of the American poet, Elizabeth Bishop (Twayne, 1966) and numerous reviews and articles. Clearly, however, she is chiefly a poet. In summing up her own achievement she says, 'It is important to me that my poetry *sound* like poetry. Although I am always conscious of having something to say in every poem, the music comes before the idea, or rather, the idea grows out of the music. Poetry differs from prose by virtue of its rhythmic pulse. Its authenticity cannot be defined, but only felt.'

The Crush

Handsome as D'Artagnan,
inaccessible as Mr Darcy,
she observes him in the bulge of her
mother's teapot . . . once.
There are other views. Church.
He, robed in the choir. She
behind hats, among pews.
Her eyes grope towards him,
swerve, avoid the
impossible terror of his attention.
Weekdays she wanders near his house.
He pounds the piano.
The *Fantasiestücke* weigh within her
like a dangerous possession.

The Sun Appears in November

When trees are bare,
when ground is more glowing than summer,
in sun, in November,
you can see what lay under
confusing eloquence of green.

Bare boughs in their cunning
twist this way and that way
trying to persuade by crooked reasoning.
But trees are constrained from within
to conform to skeleton.

Nothing they put on
will equal these lines of cold branches,
the willows in bunches,
birches like lightning,
transparent in brown spinneys, beeches.

North Sea off Carnoustie

You know it by the northern look of the shore,
by the salt-worried faces,
by an absence of trees, an abundance of lighthouses.
It's a serious ocean.

Along marram-scarred, sandbitten margins
wired roofs straggle out to where
a cold little holiday fair
has floated in and pitched itself
safely near the prairie of the golf course.
Coloured lights are sunk deep into the solid wind,
but all they've caught is a pair of lovers
and three silly boys.
Everyone else has a dog.
Or a room to get to.

The smells are of fish and of sewage and cut grass.
Oystercatchers, doubtful of habitation,
clamour 'weep, weep, weep' as they fuss over
scummy black rocks the tide leaves for them.

The sea is as near as we come to another world.

But there in your stony and windswept garden
a blackbird is confirming the grip of the land.
'You, you,' he murmurs, dark purple in his voice.

And now in far quarters of the horizon
lighthouses are awake, sending messages –
invitations to the landlocked,
warnings to the experienced,
but to anyone returning from the planet ocean,
candles in the windows of a safe earth.

ANNE STEVENSON

With my Sons at Boarhills

Gulls think it is for them
that the wormy sand rises,
brooding on its few rights,
losing its war with water.

The mussel flats ooze out,
and now the barnacled, embossed
stacked rocks are pedestals for strangers,
for my own strange sons,
scraping in the pool,
imperilling their pure reflections.

Their bodies are less beautiful than
blue heaven's pleiades of herring gulls,
or gannets, or that sloop's sail
sawtoothing the sea as if its
scenery were out of date, as if its
photographs had all been taken:
two boys left naked in a sloughed off summer,
skins and articulate backbones,
fossils for scrapbook or cluttered mantelpiece.

If you look now, quickly and askance,
you can see how the camera's eye
perfected what was motion and chance before
it clicked on this day and childhood snapshot,
scarcely seen beside
hunched rugby stripes and ugly uniforms –
shy, familiar grins in a waste of faces.

My knee joints ache and crack
as I kneel to my room's fire, feeding it.
Steam wreathes from my teacup, clouding
the graduate, the lieutenant, the weddings,
the significant man of letters, the politician
smiling from his short victory . . .

Faces I washed and scolded, only
watched as my each child laboured from his own womb,
bringing forth, without me, men who must
call me mother, love or reassess me
as their barest needs dictate, return
dreaming, rarely to this saltpool in memory,
naked on a morning full of see-through jellyfish,
with the tide out and the gulls out
grazing on healed beaches,
while sea-thrift blazes by the dry path,
and the sail stops cutting the water to pieces
and heads for some named port inland.

Their voices return like footprints over the sandflats,
permanent, impermanent, salt and sensuous
as the sea is, in its frame, its myth.

Mallaig Harbour Resembles Heaven in Spring Sunlight

Reach Mallaig and discover
Heaven is real.
Herring stir the harbour
into haloes of seagulls, or else
birds in free, dissonant chorus
are themselves white angels.

The ships glide in gracefully,
souls assured of their salvation,
not pretty
but exclusive and competent.

A work-a-day place. We should have known it.
How could we have imagined it other
than as home for the unimpeded,
the locality of accomplishment?

ANNE STEVENSON

Poem to my Daughter

'I think I'm going to have it,'
I said, joking between pains.
The midwife rolled competent
sleeves over corpulent milky arms.
'Dear, you never have it,
we deliver it.'
A judgement years proved true.
Certainly I've never had you

as you still have me, Caroline.
Why does a mother need a daughter?
Heart's needle – hostage to fortune –
freedom's end. Yet nothing's more perfect
than that bleating, razor-shaped cry
that delivers a mother to her baby.
The bloodcord snaps that held
their sphere together. The child,
tiny and alone, creates the mother.

A woman's life is her own
until it is taken away
by a first particular cry.
Then she is not alone
but a part of the premises
of everything there is.
A branch, a tide . . . a war.
When we belong to the world
we become what we are.

ANNE STEVENSON

If I Could Paint Essences

Another day in March. Late
rawness and wetness. I hear my mind say,
if only I could paint essences . . .

such as the mudness of mud
on this rainsoaked dyke where coltsfoot
displays its yellow misleading daisy;

such as the westness of west here
in England's last thatched, rivered
county. Red ploughland. Green pasture.

Black cattle. Quick water. Overpainted
by lightshafts from layered gold
and purple cumulus. A cloudness of clouds

which are not like anything but clouds.

But just as I arrive at true sightness of seeing,
unexpectedly I want to play on those bell-toned
cellos of delicate not-quite-flowering larches

that offer on the opposite hill their unfurled
amber instruments – floating, insubstantial, a rising
horizon of music embodied in light.

And in such imaginings I lose sight of sight.
Just as I will lose the tune of what
hurls in my head, as I turn back, turn

home to you, conversation, the inescapable ache
of trying to catch, say, the catness of cat
as he crouches, stalking his shadow,

on the other side of the window.

ANNE STEVENSON

Green Mountain, Black Mountain

I

White pine, sifter of sunlight,
Wintering host in New England woods,
Cold scent, icicle to the nostril,
Path without echo, unmarked page.

    I formed you, you forget me,
    I keep you like a fossil.
    The air is full of footprints.
    Rings of the sycamore spell you.
    Your name spills out on April ground
        with October leafmould . . .

Beechbole, cheekbone of the interior,
Sugaring maple, tap of sour soil,
Woody sweetness, wine of the honeybark,
Mountain trickle, bitter to the tongue.

    You acquired me out of wilderness,
    Grey maples streaked with birches,
    With your black-shuttered
    White wooden houses flanked with porches,
    Your black-painted peeling front doors.

Pairs of shuttered windows,
Sheltered lives.
Child's work, the symmetry,
Thin graves for narrow souls.

    Terra there was before *Terra Nova*.
    You brought to my furred hills
    Axes, steeples; your race split
    Hugely on the heave of the Atlantic . . .

In April the earth serves patiently its purpose.
Trees unclench their closed crimson fists
Against return. How many weeks before ease will annul
These dark, matted, snow-beaten scraps of mowin?

Dry wind-eaten beechleaves
Flutter under their birth arch.
Steeplebush and blackberry
Stoop to beginnings.

Green mountain with its shadow future,
Unwritten days in the buried stone.
Black mountain, colour of roots,
Clay in the roof, gag to the mouth.

II

In border Powys, a landrover
stalls on a hilltrack.
A farmer gets out with a halter,
plods to a sodden field where
a mare and her colt have rolled
the wet soil of Welsh weather
all a mud-lashed winter.

Unlatching the gate, he
forces the halter on the caked
anxious head of the mare,
then leads her away to where
a plan of his own makes fast
to some spindle purpose
the fate of the three of them.

The inscrutable movements of the man
puzzle the horses, who
follow him, nevertheless,
up the piebald track,
snowdeep in drift in places,
tyre-churned with red mud.

These are the Black Mountains
where the drenched sleep of Wales
troubles King Arthur in his cave,
where invisible hankerings of the dead
trouble the farms spilled over them –
the heaped fields, graves and tales.

And he, with his brace of horses,
barker at strangers, inbreeder of races,
is Teyrnon still, or Pryderi the colt-child,
fixed without shape or time
between the ghost-pull of Annwfn –
that other world, underworld, feathering
green Wales in its word-mist –

And the animal pull of his green dunged boots,
which take him, as he takes his horses,
up a red and white track for which he has
no name. A habit. An inheritance.
A cold night's work getting lambs born.
And in the morning, again.

III

Rain in the wind
  and the green need of again
    opening in this Welsh woods.

'Vermont' I want to call it,
  'Green Mountain', rafter
    over sleepers in the black

hill of returnings, shadows
  in the dry cave
    of the happened.

At a peal of memory
  they rise in tatters, imperatives,
    the word fossils,

webs of thready handwriting,
  typewritten strata, uncut stones
    culled for the typesetters' cemeteries.

★

If you, mother, had survived
  you would have written . . .

As when we were children
  and everything was going on
    forever in New Haven

you scratched in your journal –
    It is a strange reaction but
    suddenly the war has made it
    imperative to spend time at home
    reading and being with my children.

The pen drew its meanings
  through vacancy,
    threading a history.

★

And what shall I do
  with this touchable page that has
    closed over doubt in her voice these forty years?

I set the words up on the table,
  feeling for continuities,
    tape them with my quick nail. Listen.

But her shell has buried her echo in them.
  It is small, hard, a child's tooth,
    A guilt-pebble, a time preserved like an ammonite.

Then maybe on the second
  or the third day of March
    you overhear a blackbird in a dead elm,

or a thrush singing almost before you wake,
  or you walk unexpectedly into the calm
    ravage of a riverbank

where a broken branch
   kneels into rising water to remake
      predictable green tips,

and I know that it matters
   and does not matter –
      it is you in me who lives these things.

*

We'd thought she'd want us, knowing it was cancer,
But when we went to her she winced.
Her hand became a supplicating blur
That winter, and we didn't see her much.
There was a kind of wilting away in her
As if she couldn't bear the human touch
Of voices. Or it was something more
Unkind in us . . . resentful helplessness,
A guilty anger. She was dying
At us.   Dying was accusing.

IV
After April snow,
such a green thaw.
A chiff-chaff chips a warmer home
in that cloud-cliff.
The river bulges,
flexing brown Japanese muscles,
moving its smooth planes in multitudes.
Threads of white melt stitch
the slashed flanks of the hill fields.

Soon the animal will be well again,
hunting and breeding
in grass-covered bones.
It peers from these clinical windows
apprehensive but healing.
To be whole would be enough.
To be whole and well and warm,
content with a kill.

V

Crossing the Atlantic. That child-pure
impulse of away, retreating
to our God-forgetting present

from the God-rot of old Boston and Leyden.
'To remove to some other place
for sundry weighty and solid reasons.'

And then to be the letter of the place,
the page of the Lord's approval, within
the raw green misery of the risk.

'For there they should be liable to
famine and nakedness
and the want, in a manner, of all things.'

Without things, then, the thing was to be done,
the mountain changed, the chance
regiven. Taken again.

★

Crossing the Atlantic. Passport,
briefcase, two trays full of cellophane food
and a B grade film.

No, father, I mean
across to the America
that lives in the film of my mind.

You would have to be
alive there, distilled
on the spool of your life,

not as a photograph –
unhappiness or happiness staring
from the onceness of a time –

but as the living practice of a now,
   rehearsed as certain habits and expressions –
      your shoulders' loosened stoop to the piano,

or the length of you decanted on a chair,
   animate in argument, ash scattered
      from your cigarette like punctuation.

I think of the goodness of the house,
   the companionable presences of cellos
      punished in the corners like children,

or gleaming like the muscle-backs of girls,
   smug in the enslavement of one lover
      or another since the eighteenth century

made its music bread and water
   for the likes of us who,
      having no other faith,

still kept our covenant with
   foreign Bach, with Schubert,
      after-dinner Mozart, Razumovskis . . .

(The Polish ghettos
   drained into the cattle cars.
      Dying Vienna bled us violins.)

And yet through those
   immortal-seeming summers,
      music, that rare mediant window,

was glass through which we grew,
   a grace we had not
      guilt enough to refuse.

★

Chestnut blossom with its crimson stigmata,
Stamen-thrust from confused hands –
Five white petals, multiple in a
Competing order, so that each candlelabrum stands
As a tree of defeats around a *pietà* . . .

To be as one mother in a storm of sons,
The charred faces and cracked skulls of a
Comfortable century. Petal-white sands
Made of tiny shellfish. The crashed motorcycle
Where the sea withdraws with no grief at all.

VI

In dread of the black mountain.
Gratitude for the green mountain.
In dread of the green mountain,
Gratitude for the black mountain.

In dread of the fallen lintel and the ghosted hearth,
  gratitude for the green mountain.
In dread of the crying missile and the jet's chalk,
  gratitude for the black mountain.

In dread of the titled thief, thigh-deep in his name,
  gratitude for the green mountain.
In dread of the neon street to the armed moon,
  gratitude for the black mountain.

In dread of the gilded bible and the rod-cut hand,
  gratitude for the green mountain.
In dread of the uncrossed boards behind the blazing man,
  gratitude for the black mountain.

★

In dread of my shadow on the Green Mountain,
Gratitude for this April of the Black Mountain,
As the grass fountains out of its packed roots,
And a thrush repeats the repertoire of his threats:

I hate it, I hate it, I hate it.
Go away. Go away.
I will not, I will not, I will not.
Come again. Come again.

Swifts twist on the syllables of the wind currents.

Blackbirds are the cellos of the deep farms.

The Garden

She feels it like a shoulder of hair,
the garden, shrugging off the steamed, squeezed
eye of her kitchen window. Self-engendered chaos,
milky convolvulus, huge comet daisies. Tear
open the stocking of the leek pod and it frees
mathematically its globe, its light radiants.

But still she feels it hateful, August in its sweat,
the children filthy and barefoot . . . angry woman
in a stained striped apron, sipping juice off a knife,
thick syrups of pounded rose hip and pulped fruit.
In bright air, between briar roses and a viney drain,
Arenea diadema sips the silk-spindled fly.

Her pet cat's a killer, a fur muff
curled fatly now in a catnest of hot
grass and goutweed. Of this morning's robin
too much was left – feathers, fluff
feet, beak, the gorgeous throat caught
in the gored, delicate, perfectly balanced skeleton.

Swifts

Spring comes a little, a little. All April it rains.
The new leaves stick in their fists. New ferns, still fiddleheads.
But one day the swifts are back. Face to the sun like a child
You shout, 'The swifts are back!'

Sure enough, bolt nocks bow to carry one sky-scyther
Two hundred miles an hour across fullblown windfields.
Swreeeee. Swreeee. Another. And another.
It's the cut air falling in shrieks on our chimneys and roofs.

The next day, a fleet of high crosses cruises in ether.
These are the air pilgrims, pilots of air rivers . . .
But a shift of wing and they're earth-skimmers, daggers,
Skilful in guiding the throw of themselves away from
themselves.

Quick flutter, a scimitar upsweep, out of danger of touch, for
Earth is forbidden to them, water's forbidden to them.
All air and fire, little owlish ascetics, they outfly storms.
They rush to the pillars of altitude, the thermal fountains.

Here is a legend of swifts, a parable –
When the great Raven bent over earth to create the birds
The swifts were ungrateful. They were small muddy things
Like shoes, with long legs and short wings, so

They took themselves off to the mountains to sulk.
And they stayed there. 'Well,' said the Raven, after years of this,
'I will give you the sky, you can have the whole sky
On condition that you give up rest.'

'Yes, yes,' screamed the swifts. 'We abhor rest.
We detest the filth of growth, the sweat of sleep,
Soft nests in the wet fields, slimehold of worms.
Let us be free, be air!'

So the Raven took their legs and bound them into their bodies.
He bent their wings like boomerangs, honed them like knives.
He streamlined their feathers and stripped them of velvet.
Then he released them, *Never to Return*

Inscribed on their feet and wings. And so
We have swifts, though in reality not parables but
Bolts in the world's need, swift
Swifts, not in punishment, not in ecstasy, simply

Sleepers over oceans in the mill of the world's breathing.
The grace to say they live in another firmament.
A way to say the miracle will not occur,
And watch the miracle.

NOTES

Edward Brathwaite

The Emigrants

In *Rights of Passage*, from which this extract is taken, Brathwaite remembers different types of emigrant. He switches from describing poor Negroes arriving today at 'sea-port quays' or airports to describing Columbus on his first voyage to the West Indies. As Columbus' ship approached various West Indian islands (before he made his first landing at San Salvador, near the Bahamas, in the northern part of the West Indies), he saw the tropical plants and crabs that he expected to see, but he did not foresee that his crew would start the killing of the Caribs, the original natives who lived in the West Indies before Europeans arrived, and who were almost wiped out.

Brathwaite highlights the immediacy of past events by using whichever tense suits him, and by introducing himself into past events, such as when he says 'I watched him (i.e. Columbus) pause'.

This extract from *Rights of Passage* reveals Brathwaite's sympathy for West Indian emigrants looking for jobs in North America and Europe today; later it also reveals Brathwaite's intense feeling for the texture of the islands where he was brought up, and beyond which Columbus sailed. Brathwaite is keenly aware of the structure of the islands, and the distinctive appearance of their birds, waterfalls, seashores, rivers and trees. He is also eager to emphasise the continuity between the past and present of the islands. He feels unable to escape from his ancestry and is searching for the nature of his roots. He is aware of the various ways in which the original life of the islands has been destroyed by the arrival of the Europeans, and he thinks of Columbus as an intruder, sailing *through my summer air* to *touch our land*. He feels all the evil, cruel experiences that have been suffered by the coloured inhabitants, whether Carib or Negro, as happening to himself; he feels that the cruel overseer who kicked a Negro slave at some point in time between 1492 and 1969 had tipped his black boot into *my belly*.

l. 2 *grips:* travelling-bags, suit-cases.

l. 25 *painfields:* the Mississippi cotton fields where the Negroes endured pain as they worked.

l. 40 *kaffirs:* literally this word means the poor Negroes living in South Africa, but Brathwaite uses it to refer to all poor Negroes. 'Columbus coursing Kaffirs' means poor Negroes who are imitating Columbus by emigrating.

l. 41 The *Cathay shores* that the emigrants seek literally refer to China; but here they mean some idealised, romantic, distant country that the emigrants hope will satisfy their ambitions and longings. In reality their actual experience of foreign countries will seem disappointing to them after their rosy expectations.

l. 70 *pouis:* a flowering shrub that grows prolifically in the West Indies.

Leopard

In this extract from *Islands* Brathwaite uses the leopard as a symbol of the spirit of the West Indian peoples who were free in the past, just as the leopard was; once they were great, and they hope to return to their true place of importance in the world.

l. 23 The *antelope* and the *duiker* are similar animals. They are two types of small deer that are the natural prey of the leopard in Africa.

l. 85 *anealed:* anointed with oil and so prepared ritually for death.

South

This extract is from *Rights of Passage*. Brathwaite is describing the sunny beaches of his birthplace, the island of Barbados in the south-east of the West Indies. Here he paints an idealised picture of an unchanging world.

Ogun

Brathwaite's uncle is an old-fashioned craftsman, obstinately persisting with an old skill that is threatened by imported cabinets and similar products of mechanised carpentry overseas. But Brathwaite has given his uncle the name of an African god, the creator god who is seen as a divine craftsman. He imagines that when his uncle worked as a carpenter and wood-carver in the West Indies he was subconsciously carrying on the work of the Africans who made wooden masks of the god Ogun. Brathwaite is resolved to trace the continuity by which certain aspects of African culture survived in the West Indies among the slaves whose ancestors had been shipped there from Africa. He tries to calculate, especially in his long poem *Rights of Passage*, how much the Negroes in the New World have kept, or even recreated, of their African past. He is repeatedly trying to answer the question of the rich old lady who asked him on one of his visits to Europe:

> 'Have you no language of your own
> No way of doing things?
> Did you spend all those holidays
> At England's apron strings?'

Littoral

The title-word means 'concerning the shore'. In this poem Barbadian society is likened to an old, blind fisherman who has rich memories of a heroic past symbolised as a woman. But their hopes of happiness did not materialise. Extremists and fanatics (e.g. the *Quaker* of l. 65 and the slaves of l. 69) combined to destroy the vitality of the islanders and the beauty of the island.

l. 41 *immanent:* indwelling, inherent. (Sometimes Brathwaite plays on both the sounds and meanings of words, so he may be using the word *immanent* to mean both immanent and imminent.)

Twine

This extract from Brathwaite's *Mother Poem* illustrates his distinctive use of words. He uses pronouns in the way that they are used in colloquial West Indian speech. For instance, in l. 2 and l. 6 the nominative form *he* is used when the accusative form *him* would be more usual; even *e* is used instead of *him*. In using nouns Brathwaite may use the singular instead of the plural (e.g. l. 20) and vice versa.

l.9 *excursion train:* from 1881 to 1937 a simple railway connected the main sugar-growing areas of the island with its port and city. Apart from the economic uses of the line, it provided the poor workers with cheap trips to the sea.

l. 24 *chess:* a Creole form of the word *chest.*

ll. 24–25 *steel donkey:* very noisy donkey engine.

1. 28 *crackle:* left-overs.

l. 36 *trash:* comparatively useless matter, rubbish, sugar cane plants and leaves from which the most valuable part has been removed, and which can be used as fuel.

l. 45 *poor backra:* Backra is an Afro-Caribbean word for the white man, but the *poor backra* are the descendants of white peasants introduced into Barbados in the seventeenth century. These servants still survive as a distinct ethnic group, and were never slaves in the full sense of the word.

Islands

In *Islands*, an extract from a longer poem with the same name, Brathwaite is saying that one can take either a kindly or an unkindly view of the West Indian islands, but there will be no progress unless the people act more hopefully and positively.

l. 17 The *Antilles* islands form an archipelago near Jamaica, in the southern part of the West Indies.

ll. 48–49 Brathwaite habitually turns past and present into one unity. So he treats the fact that the slave-owners used to brand their slaves like cattle as though it were an important present-day truth.

l. 53 *Antigua* is in the eastern sector of the West Indies, north of Barbados and Trinidad.

The New Ships

This is an extract from *Masks*, in which Brathwaite returns to Africa, from which his ancestors were shipped as slaves.

l. 1 *Takoradi:* a twentieth-century port built in the 1920s in Ghana.

l. 4 *Laterite:* a red, friable clay, containing iron; it is often used for roadmaking in the tropics.

ll. 16–21 Brathwaite is reporting the journey of his ancestors (from Ghana to the West Indies) in reverse.

ll. 37–38 *flintlocks:* an old-fashioned type of rifle.

Charles Causley

'HMS Glory' at Sydney

Causley, at home in Cornwall, remembers visiting Sydney Harbour a few days before World War II ended, when he was a member of the crew of the aircraft-carrier *HMS Glory*. Sydney Harbour is a long, complicated inlet, inside a narrow opening in the cliffs.

l. 4 The *Blue Mountains* are east of Sydney, so the sun that rises on them would be visible in the city.

l. 9 The bridge appears so suddenly that it looks like a bridge in a painting by Whistler. Whistler (1834–1903) was an American painter who lived for most of his life in England. He painted striking impressionistic pictures of bridges across the River Thames, e.g. Old Battersea Bridge.

l. 12 The *Solomons*: a group of islands in the Pacific which are comparatively near to Australia.

l. 16 There is a little irony or coincidence in the fact that the pilot-boat that comes to help them find the best route into Sydney harbour is named after Captain Cook, the first European navigator to explore most of the Australian coast. Incidentally he never actually entered Sydney harbour, though he landed at Botany Bay which is very near to Sydney.

l. 27 *Liberty men:* sailors with official permission to go ashore.

l. 34 *Castlereagh Street:* the circular bar was in Usher's Hotel, which was once a popular night spot, but has since been pulled down.

l. 36 *schooners:* tall beer glasses.

l. 39 *beer engines:* pumps for dispensing beer.

l. 42 *matelots:* a colloquial word for sailors.

ll. 41–47 Causley's question to Janie ends at *flowers*. With the next words, *Across three continents*, he begins to address both Janie and the city of Sydney.

l. 56 *Woolloomoolloo:* an industrial area in Sydney, once a red light district, but now growing in respectability.

l. 74 *Q:* Quiller-Couch (1863–1944) was a famous novelist who lived in Cornwall, Causley's native county. His works include *From a Cornish Window*.

l. 79 *La Perouse:* the use of this French word for the prison in Sydney reminds us that French seamen played an important part in early explorations of the Pacific.

Chief Petty Officer

The Chief Petty Officer (i.e. non-commissioned officer) of a Royal Naval Barracks would be a formidable person, responsible for administration and discipline, especially in relation to recruits. He despises *hostilities-only ratings*, i.e. those who have joined the Navy only for the duration of the war. Causley's description of him is a parody of Walter Pater's description of the Mona Lisa in Leonardo da Vinci's painting, which begins: 'She is older than the rocks among which she sits: like the vampire, she has been dead many times, and learned the secrets of the grave; and has been a diver in deep seas, and keeps their fallen day about her . . .'

l. 7 *Nirvana:* heaven.

l. 15 *Crippen:* Crippen, an Edwardian murderer, wore a formal collar. He fled to the USA, but was the first criminal to be brought back to England for trial as a result of the fact that the ship he was travelling on had an early radio set.

l. 20 *WRNS:* the women's branch of the Royal Navy.

l. 26 The Chief Petty Officer is guilty of bad grammar in that he has mixed up the transitive verb to *lay* and the intransitive verb to *lie*.

l. 33 The ancient Greek conqueror, Alexander, took his army from Europe to Egypt, Persia and India, and presumably became very sun-burnt.

l. 38 *pusser's clock:* a clock that is official Navy issue and so has been issued by a purser, an officer who keeps the ship's accounts and issues official stores.

l. 40 The Chief Petty Officer had fought at the Battle of Jutland, which occurred off the Danish coast and was the main confrontation between the British and German battle fleets in the First World War.

Yelverton

The land climbs steeply if one travels northwards, and therefore inland, from the outskirts of Plymouth to such towns as Yelverton. Further north one reaches places like Princetown (where the prison is) that are actually on Dartmoor.

l. 7 *sick-bay tiffies:* sick-berth attendants.

l. 7 *the Mongolian Chief Yeomen:* non-commissioned officers similar in age and responsibility to the Chief Petty Officer whom Causley describes in the previous poem. Their faces look as expressionless as those of Mongolians.

Death of an Aircraft

In 1941 the Germans invaded Crete, which was then regarded as part of Greece, and was defended unsuccessfully by the British as well as the Greeks. The campaign was remarkable for the large-scale use of paratroops by the Germans and for the bitter ferocity with which the campaign was fought, especially between the Germans and the natives of Crete.

l. 12 *sauerkraut:* a dish of chopped pickled cabbage which Causley regards as a typical item of German food.

l. 47 *raki:* the Turkish version of ouzo, the favourite form of alcohol in Greece; raki is a liqueur made from Cretan grapes.

l. 63 Causley means that the Greek took the decisive step of becoming a combatant guerrilla soldier, but he has chosen an odd metaphor since in the eighteenth century an Englishman who accepted a silver shilling from a recruiting sergeant accepted the legal fact that he had become a member of a professional army.

Ballad for Katharine of Aragon

This poem is a lament for the death of Causley's friend, Jumper Cross, who was killed at the age of twenty-seven and a half, as well as for the death of Queen Katharine of Aragon. Line 44 reminds the reader that Katharine reigned as queen for twenty-four years (1509 to 1533). Henry VIII reigned for a long time before he grew tired of her and began to believe that God had not approved of their marriage.

l. 6 *the Flying Scot:* a famous steam train which ran between Edinburgh and King's Cross, London, and so went past Peterborough Cathedral.

l. 33 *party:* a naval slang word for a girl.

At the Grave of John Clare

This is one of a small group of poems that reflect Causley's knowledge of the area around Peterborough, where he was a student. John Clare (1793–1864) was born at Helpston, a village just north-west of Peterborough. Maxey is just north of Helpston.

At the beginning of his career as a poet, Clare gained considerable notoriety, since it was unusual in the early 1830s for a farm labourer to publish poetry. But later his patrons, and his literary friends such as Lamb and Hazlitt, seemed to lose interest in him and he went mad – chiefly from disappointment. For some years a nobleman who had been impressed by Clare's poetry paid an annual sum for him to receive slightly better treatment than was normally meted out to lunatics, but one would never deduce this from the poems that Clare wrote in the madhouse, which include such lines as 'My friends forsake me like a memory lost'.

When Clare died he was buried at Helpston. A monument to him stands at the cross-roads in the middle of the village.

l. 11 *Dutch landscape:* Helpston is at the edge of the East Anglian fens, a flat landscape which resembles Holland.

Timothy Winters

l. 14 *Suez Street:* the name of the street suggests that the houses in it were being built during the nineteenth century, at the same time as the Suez Canal was being constructed.

l. 25 *belves:* the schoolmaster makes a desperate, pleading note like that of a cow who has been separated from her calf.

Tony Connor

The Poet's District

At times the present tense refers, as in line 1, to the adult poet thinking now; at other times it refers to the boy, playing some version of hare and hounds or tig, in which he runs away from his pursuers and then hides until they find him.

ll. 3–4 He cannot escape thinking about, and remembering, the entries – i.e. narrow passage-ways between houses in a built-up urban area. Entries are sometimes called 'ginnels'.

l. 8 *limbos:* forgotten dark areas like the outskirts of hell.

ll. 13–15 By the rules of the game that they were playing, young Connor had to leave marks on the wall as some help to his pursuers.

l. 17 *brews:* steep slopes, especially in paths and minor roads.
crofts: In Greater Manchester this means pieces of rough open ground.

l. 19 *ginnels:* narrow passage-ways between yards or houses, very similar to *entries.*

l. 20 *privies:* outside lavatories.

October in Clowes Park

Such parks are a characteristic feature of Britain's industrial towns. This particular one is in Salford, now part of Greater Manchester.

Connor is genuinely angry that our industrial society has made this area so ugly and dirty, yet he remembers that he enjoyed playing in the park as a boy and he notices how happy are today's children playing in the park's pear tree.

ll. 8–9 *arrow* is a verb, and *shutting* means *welding.*

l. 16 *swags:* just as a burglar acquires swag, so the gardens of the buildings just outside the park have acquired a few trees.

The Burglary

l. 48 *tumblers:* part of the mechanism of locks.

My Mother's Husband

l. 37 *Lohengrin:* an opera by Wagner.

Lodgers

l. 11 *Unwitting fathers:* they did not realise that they had become father figures for the young Connor whose real father had left home.

Druid's Circle

Between 2000 and 1000 BC the inhabitants of Britain built circles of large stones of which Stonehenge is the best known example. The circles probably had some connection with both religion and astronomy. They are usually found on minor hills with impressive views. Possibly the weather was a little warmer when they were constructed. During the last three hundred years many people have imagined, quite wrongly, that they were built by the Druids, Celtic priests who did not arrive in Britain until a few years before the Roman invasion. Moreover many people have imagined, without any evidence, that these circles were associated with human sacrifices. Names such as 'the sacrificial stone' have been given to particular stones, with no evidence.

l. 4 Auschwitz, Belsen and Buchenwald were Nazi concentration camps.

Above Penmaenmawr

Penmaenmawr is a town on the coast of north Wales, west of Llandudno. Behind it the mountains rise quickly towards Snowdonia. For instance, the ridge of Talyfan, not far inland, is 2,000 ft (nearly 700 metres) above sea level.

Douglas Dunn

The Clothes Pit

ll. 8–11 These young women do not need to carry a copy of a fashionable paper in order to impress other people. They live in an unfashionable street in Hull.

The New Girls

l. 15 *at fifty:* having dropped the girls, the men drive away at a speed that seems like 50 mph. *They* in line 16 refers to the girls again.

Under the Stone

ll. 14–15 During most of the years from 1815 to the present day the capitalist countries often suffered from economic depressions, periods of a few years in which unemployment grew and the ruling classes brought cavalry into the streets to repress protests by the poor.

l. 16 They are almost meaningless and insignificant. We see them only on a few unusual occasions, like slugs that live under stones.

Guerrillas

The last two lines of this poem explain the title. Dunn thinks of guerrillas as fighters who will use any weapons that they can get, but who usually have to make do with knives. Usually too they have a social or nationalist grudge. Dunn says that the children who had not been born into farming families felt that their ancestors had been robbed of their share of the land, and so these children inherited the sense of grievance that is as typical of the guerrillas as their knives. The poem is told from the point of view of the guerrillas, and the word *they* in line 1 refers to the privileged families.

The Competition

l. 6 *coup:* manure cart.

l. 12 *Hurricane:* an English fighter-plane used in World War II.

l. 16 Young Dunn had never realised until then that his dress and appearance would make him seem poor to upper-class boys.

l. 17 *cried:* exclaimed.

Boys with Coats

l. 8 A Fleet Air Arm aerodrome would have the same sort of name as a warship, so its name is *HMS Sanderling*.

l. 21 He felt he was a *radical*, i.e. someone who wanted social reform. He thought that the passengers on the bus, who supported the conductress in excluding the boy with no coat, had been guilty of a major injustice. He was bitterly disappointed that his own gesture in giving the poor boy his pocket money and his model aeroplane (the Hurricane) had achieved so little.

White Fields

The poem moves to and fro between Dunn as a boy of six having a nightmare in 1948, and the mature Dunn writing the poem quite recently. He is appalled to think how much cruelty was perpetrated in the world during the first six years of his life, during which his mother tried to conceal the truth about the world from him and from herself. Rather harshly he rejects her well-meant dishonesty in line 36 ('I reject Your generation') and suggests that *Everybody's*, a popular weekly during the war, was equally resolved to forget the cruellest truths.

The House Next Door

The two ladies live next door, but Dunn has imagined an unpublished play, written by himself, which exaggerates their oddities. Freddie Lonsdale (line 3) was a successful dramatist in the 1920s, who wrote comedies similar to those of Somerset Maugham and Ben Travers. His comedy, *The Last of Mrs Cheyney*, about a beautiful young woman who turns crook, is often revived today.

Irving Berlin (line 17) was born in 1888 in the USA. He was a successful and prolific writer of popular music, including favourite tunes such as 'Alexander's Ragtime Band' and the musical comedy *Call Me Madam*.

Ships

l. 4 *malefic:* harmful.

Washing the Coins

l. 34 *howkers:* tattie-howker is a Scots dialect word for a man who digs up potatoes.

Seamus Heaney

The Wife's Tale

Her husband and his reapers have stacked up the corn in a field and are threshing it before they put the corn into bags and the straw into barns.

l. 12 *I declare a woman could lay out a field:* in a mood of teasing admiration he is paying her a compliment. To lay out a field is to prepare it for display and make it impressive to look at.

Churning Day

A butter-churn is made of wood and is shaped like a barrel. It is set on a stand so that the churn itself can be revolved by hand. When the lid is fitted, the wooden spatulas or blades agitate the cream inside the churn so that it forms clots on its sides, thus making butter. As soon as Heaney's mother had made one instalment of butter, all the equipment had to be sterilised with boiling water, so that the apparatus could be used successfully next time. The newly-formed butter was removed from the churn and wooden instruments – similar to spades – were used to shape it into oblong slabs. These 'spades' often had a decorative pattern which made the pounds of butter look more attractive.

l. 2 *crocks:* earthenware pots used in the making of butter.

l. 4 *the hot brewery:* this line describes how the cow's body produces warm milk.

l. 7 *plumping kettles:* unusually large ones.

l. 12 *the staff:* its function resembled that of an agitator in a washing-machine.
muddler: a churning stick for crushing and mixing the ingredients.

l. 27 *the house would stink:* the smell of sour milk would persist, e.g. in the cloths they had used.

l. 31 *gravid:* literally this word means *pregnant*; but here it refers to the optimistic expectancy of the churners, who believed that the long and chancy process of churning would finally produce cream on the surface of the buttermilk and then turn it into butter.

Thatcher

l. 1 *bespoke:* booked and engaged in advance.
l. 7 *flicked:* shaken in the air – so that their weight could be tested.
l. 9 *honed:* sharpened on a whetstone.
l. 11 *staple:* he turned the white twig into a curved 'nail' that held the bundles of straw in position.
l. 14 *butts:* the thicker ends of the hazel and willow rods.
l. 16 *Midas:* in Greek mythology, King Midas turned everything that he touched into gold.

Digging

l. 10 *lug:* the projecting part of the main section of a spade.
l. 22 *nicking:* making indentations.

Storm on the Island

ll. 17–19 The words *strafes*, *salvo* and *bombarded* carry on the same metaphor, and suggest that the wind launches a series of attacks against the island and the houses on it.

The Diviner

l. 3 *the pluck:* the sudden sharp tug that the water produces in the diviner's forked twig.

Ted Hughes

Hawk Roosting

Hughes said that 'the poem of mine usually cited for violence is the one about the Hawk Roosting, this drowsy hawk sitting in a wood and talking to itself. That bird is accused of being a fascist ... the symbol of some horrible totalitarian dictator'. Hughes went on to say that he was thinking of the Creator and Nature when he wrote the poem, but he lets them express their thoughts through the words of a hawk. Poems such as this led the critic A. E. Dyson to conclude that 'the major theme' in Hughes' poems is power.

Yet it is unusual in Hughes' early poetry for him to make a bird or animal the narrator. Usually Hughes himself is the narrator of the poem and a minor character in it.

l. 2 *no falsifying dream:* the hawk is unlike man, whose thoughts and self-consciousness prevent his arms and feet from doing at once what his head tells them to do.

l. 15 *sophistry:* an attempt at reasoning that seems convincing but is really false. The hawk believes himself superior to man, who is often misled by sophistry.

Pike

Hughes has recorded that he used to be a keen angler for pike, especially in the very deep and very old pond that he envisages in this poem. He was fascinated by the huge pike who lived, he believed, at a great depth in it; they were only occasionally seen and then only as vague shapes like sunken railway sleepers.

Hughes realises that what is horrible about them is the pitch of specialisation that these pike have reached as killers, as though they existed solely for their jaws to eat their prey: they have 'a life subdued to its instrument'. Pike eat their own kind as a matter of course. They often grow to a huge size, and one even weighed 90 lbs.

In the end Hughes goes fishing at night, not for pike, but for some nameless horror.

l. 16 *pectorals:* fins.

Crow Hears Fate Knock on the Door

l. 14 *gobbets:* pieces of flesh that had been torn from the carcase of the mole.

The Horses

This poem is a good example of the fact that not all Hughes' poems are about predators; but the horses in this poem share the stillness of the hawk as it perches in a high tree. The poem begins with the world whitened by frost an hour before dawn. The horses are as still as megaliths, the large stones used to build such monuments as Stonehenge. From the ridge of the moor Hughes watches the sun rise, with explosive suddenness. He feels that he has within himself no real heat to match the sun's, only a restless fever. But he believes that a memory of the patience of those horses as they wait for the dawn will help him to face the problems of life.

ll. 16–34 Hughes regards the horses as more in tune with the landscape than he is. He listens in *emptiness* and is *stumbling*, whereas the horses remain *patient*. They are not disturbed by the sudden, melodramatic appearance of the sun – as Hughes has been.

The Warm and the Cold

l. 29 *tide-rip:* rough water caused by opposing tides.
l. 34 *score of a jig:* the lost music of a lively dance.

The Retired Colonel

Like the last wolf to survive in England, and the last sturgeon to swim in the Thames before it became polluted, the retired Colonel was the last of his kind. Hughes expresses his admiration for the Colonel by comparing him to a bull. He looked as though he had been one of the defenders of Mafeking, a town in which British soldiers successfully endured a long siege during the South African (Boer) War.

A remark typical of those made by Hughes' hostile critics was made by the Scottish poet, Alan Bold, about this poem: 'Hughes would substitute for our "pimply age" – if *he* paid more attention to the headlines he would find our age far from "pimply" – an icebound battleground on which Dick Straightup would no doubt outdrink the pike, and the Retired Colonel would do battle with the mammoths. Hughes is more successful as an informed observer than as a mighty thinker.'

Six Young Men

Hughes is looking at a photograph of six of his father's friends, who were killed in World War I. The landscape of their part of Yorkshire had not changed much since their death – at least when Hughes wrote this poem in the 1950s. Hughes' later poetry shows how aware he has become of recent changes in the Yorkshire landscape.

Elizabeth Jennings

My Grandmother

l. 2 *Apostle spoons:* spoons with the figures of the twelve apostles on their handles.
ll. 4 and 18 Elizabeth Jennings here shows the same interest in reflections that she shows in her poem, *Mirrors.*

San Paolo Fuori le Mura, Rome

This is one of the largest and most famous of the churches in Rome. It was built outside the traditional walls of Rome, at the place where St Paul was martyred.

Philip Larkin

To the Sea

l. 20 *Famous Cricketers:* before 1939 most cigarette packets contained a card, which would be part of a series that boys collected. One series was of fifty famous cricketers.

ll. 21–22 One of his earliest memories is of his parents showing a very human interest in a quack doctor selling patent medicines on the beach.

Going, Going

This poem served as a prologue to a government report on the Human Habitat. It is the nearest that Larkin has come to writing propaganda.

l. 28 *estuaries:* presumably it will be particularly profitable to build houses or even factories near the mouths of rivers.

MCMXIV

This poem is of course about the year 1914.

l. 15 *twist:* a form of tobacco.

ll. 15–16 Licensing laws, which restrict the sale of alcohol to certain hours, chiefly date from the later years of World War I.

Homage to a Government

The statues (line 15) are of explorers and soldiers who added territories to the British Empire in the past. Larkin believes that most of them brought peace and prosperity to these territories. Many lines are ironical (e.g. 11–12) since Larkin pretends to believe the arguments that he hears and now repeats.

The Explosion

ll. 16–18 The preacher is giving his sermon at the memorial service.

ll. 19–25 Larkin interrupts the sermon to tell us that at the second when the explosion occurred the miners' wives had telepathic visions of their husbands.

Reference Back

Larkin was jazz correspondent of the *Daily Telegraph* and wrote a book called *All What Jazz*. In this poem he is talking to his mother, the *you* of line 1.

l. 7 *Oliver's* Riverside Blues: 'King' Oliver (1885–1938) was a great jazz cornet-player.

l. 10 *Chicago air:* many of the best jazz records were recorded in Chicago.

l. 12 *The year after I was born:* in 1923 King Oliver and his Creole Jazz Band made some famous recordings.

Edwin Morgan

The Old Man and the Sea

The title of the poem is a reference to the short story of that name by Ernest Hemingway (1898–1961), and the whole poem is related to Hemingway.

In Morgan's volume of poetry *The Second Life* (published by the Edinburgh University Press in 1968), he included poems about the suicides of both Ernest Hemingway and Marilyn Monroe.

The mist which Morgan describes at the beginning of *The Old Man and the Sea* is a symbol to emphasise the existence of an obscurely hostile environment. Similarly, in *Aberdeen Train*, the pheasant is surrounded by a mist as it looks at a piece of glass that glints in the autumn sun.

The Unspoken

l. 7 Kipling wrote a poem, later set to music and made into a popular song, called *Mandalay*. In this poem a former British soldier who had taken part in the original British conquest of Burma imagines his native girl friend singing:

'Come you back, you British soldier; come you back to Mandalay!
Come you back to Mandalay,
Where the old Flotilla lay:
Can't you 'ear their paddles chunkin' from Rangoon to Mandalay?
On the road to Mandalay,
Where the flyin'-fishes play,
An' the dawn comes up like thunder outer China 'crost the Bay!'

l. 16 The Russians launched their second sputnik on 3rd November, 1957. This sputnik was launched into space with a dog named Laika on board.

l. 27 In Greek mythology Prometheus stole from the gods the gift of making fire, and gave this information to mankind. So Morgan feels that the warmth in his cheeks derives from Prometheus.

Strawberries

l. 32 The Kilpatrick hills lie north-west of Glasgow, east of Dumbarton, Helensburgh and the river Clyde.

Trio

l. 2 Morgan probably sees some parallel between these three people coming up Buchanan Street bearing gifts and the three Wise Men of the Christmas story.

l. 12 Orpheus was the human musician in Greek mythology who played an instrument and sang so well that he charmed the animals.

Aberdeen Train

l. 11 The Mearns are a hilly district near Glasgow.

Ché

Ché Guevara (1928–67) was a revolutionary hero. Born in Argentina, he took part in Castro's war that won him control of Cuba. Later Guevara led a band of guerrillas in an invasion of Bolivia, then ruled by a right-wing dictatorship, but he was killed. He invented new tactics which guerrilla insurgents and left-wing propagandists have used against many right-wing governments. Ché is an Argentine word meaning 'chum'.

Starryveldt

In this poem Edwin Morgan is experimenting with concrete poetry. In other poems, not included in this anthology, he carries these experiments further; for instance, he begins a poem on bees' hives with these two lines:

> 'busybykeabloodybizzinbees
> bloodybusybykeobizzinbees'

and continues to play with words that imitate the sound of bees for twelve lines.

Concrete poetry is poetry in the form of a picture; the look of it conveys the essential meaning to the reader at once.

Since World War I various poets of different nationalities have attempted to write concrete poetry, but Morgan has been one of the most persistent exponents.

Starryveldt uses this technique to express Morgan's indignation about the regime in South Africa. At Sharpeville in 1960 the South African police fired on Negro demonstrators and killed sixty-seven people, most of whom were shot in the back as they fled.

l. 21 *voortrekker:* literally, it describes one of the Boer pioneers who left Cape Province and trekked by ox-cart to the Transvaal to get away from British rule. As metaphorical abuse the word can be applied today to people whose views on race relations are as cruel and out-of-date as those of the original Boers.

l. 29 *Vae victis* is a Latin phrase meaning 'Woe to the conquered'.

Norman Nicholson

Have You Been to London?

l. 6 *neb:* a projecting piece, e.g. the spout of a kettle or the peak of a cap.

Boo to a Goose

l. 2 *skittered:* moved like a water-bird which lands with a series of splashes.

l. 6 *coddled:* treated me like an invalid.

l. 29 *skein:* aim (as though they were aiming a knife-thrust at him).

l. 44 *lochan:* a small lake.

l. 45 *brae:* hillside.
voe-side: side of a small bay.

The Black Guillemot

l. 1 St Bees has a complex promontory with a north and a south headland, both of which face the Irish Sea.

l. 3 *Galloway:* part of Scotland, visible from Cumbria across the Solway Firth.

l. 11 *guillemots:* sea birds who nest on coastal cliffs.

l. 20 *iced:* whitened.

l. 23 *auk:* a general word for several similar kinds of sea-bird. Nicholson is referring to a black guillemot. A few pairs breed as far south as north Wales but they belong in greatest numbers to Scottish coasts.

l. 30 *lets:* intrudes.

Cleator Moor

Cleator Moor is an industrial area just inland from St Bee's Head. Formerly, both coal and iron ore (which is red in colour) were obtained from the same mine here, which was unusual. Both Cleator Moor and Egremont are about 30 miles north of Millom.

ll. 13–20 These lines refer to the slumps of 1918–39.

ll. 21–32 These lines refer to the renewed demand for coal and iron during World War II. *Wick* (line 21) means *alive* (with men).

l. 30 *segged:* swollen.

Egremont

Egremont is a small town a few miles south-east of Whitehaven and St Bee's Head, i.e. about 30 miles north of Millom. Formerly iron ore was mined here, while the ruins of the medieval castle still retain some grandeur.

l. 11 *ragwort:* a wild flower that is a kind of bright yellow daisy.

l. 12 *pinchbeck:* Nicholson combines two meanings – the colour is that of a cheap alloy used in cheap jewellery, and it is also the sort of gold that might be thrown away by a miser.

l. 46 According to tradition the Horn of Egremont can be blown only by the rightful owner of the castle.

On the Closing of Millom Ironworks
September 1968

l. 19 *in '28:* in the slump that was at its worst in 1928.

l. 28 *the 'Brew':* the bureau, i.e. the Labour Exchange. This colloquial term was widely used in the north of England and Ireland. Being 'on the brew' means being on the dole.

To the River Duddon

The river Duddon rises in the Lake District and flows towards the south-west, passing most of the places that Nicholson mentions in his poem. The Duddon eventually forms a wide, shallow estuary (with the town of Millom on its north shore) a few miles west of Barrow-in-Furness. William Wordsworth used to walk long distances among parts of the Lake District that are high and remote; for instance, Hard Knott pass is well over 1,000 ft, and was inaccessible to cars until after 1945. Wordsworth walked over Hard Knott as an old man; previously, in his middle age, he wrote a series of sonnets about the River Duddon.

l. 44 *Remote from . . . industry:* since about 1850 the western part of Cumbria has been like Hughes' West Yorkshire and D. H. Lawrence's Nottinghamshire – a place where mining and factories have spread erratically over the face of the countryside but have not destroyed all its beauty. The following line means that the river Duddon was no longer remote from industry.

On Duddon Marsh

l. 4 *on the third day:* according to Genesis I: 9–13 it was on the third day of the Creation that God divided the sea from the dry land.

St Luke's Summer

St Luke's Day is October 18th. Quite often a series of mild, sunny days occur about this time.

To the Memory of a Millom Musician

l. 14 *smut-bells:* Nicholson invents the word to link two forms of boyish humour – ringing door-bells and running away, and telling smutty stories.

l. 16 *ink-smitted:* stained and marked with ink.

l. 17 *a down-at-heel decade:* the years 1930–40, when many men and women were unemployed, especially in Cumbria.

l. 23 *moraine:* literally the mass of débris found at the end of a glacier. Just as a moraine is a dull residual deposit, so Harry Pelleymounter began to think of middle-age as a dreary anticlimax after the 1930s (despite their poverty) when he had been younger, and had been in great demand as a musician.

Old Man at a Cricket Match

Presumably the old man is a spectator at a cricket match which his village is in danger of losing. He supports the side that is batting.

Innocents' Day

Nicholson imagines Herod making excuses for his action in putting to death all the children in Bethlehem under the age of two, in an attempt to kill the newly-born Saviour of whom the Wise Men had spoken. Nicholson, of course, does not accept these excuses. The murdered children are usually referred to as the Holy Innocents.

ll. 9–10 *the occupying power:* the Romans had allowed Herod a certain amount of power to carry out their policies.

Vernon Scannell

Autumn

l. 23 *velutinous:* velvety.

Here and Human

l. 10 The words in quotation marks are from a previous author; they describe the human voice in song, in this case the operatic tenor.

August 1914

ll. 19–21 In 1919, when the world had been *wounded* by World War I the Frenchman Georges Carpentier knocked out the Englishman, Joe Becket, in a contest for the heavy-weight championship of the world.

Gunpowder Plot

l. 28 *John* is the name of the first boy, who speaks in l.13.

Anne Stevenson

The Crush

l. 1 *D'Artagnan:* one of the musketeers in a novel by Dumas.

l. 2 *Mr Darcy:* the hero of *Pride and Prejudice* by Jane Austen. Brought up as a proud member of an aristocratic family, he found it difficult to be friendly and sociable with people whom he considered to belong to a lower class.

l. 13 *Fantasiestücke:* the kind of romantic musical composition that would be written by a nineteenth-century German composer such as Schumann.

North Sea off Carnoustie

Carnoustie is on Scotland's east coast, just north of the Firth of Tay.

l. 5 *marram:* a shore grass that binds sand.

l. 16 *oyster-catchers:* conspicuous wading birds that live near most coasts of northern Britain. They have black and white plumage, orange-red bills and red legs. Anne Stevenson describes their cry as 'weep, weep, weep', which is very similar to the noisy cry of 'kleep-kleep' which the RSPB ascribes to them in its *Guide to British Birds.*

l. 27 Anne Stevenson thinks that the ocean is divided as distinctly from the land as though it were another *planet.*

With my Sons at Boarhills

Boarhills is near the coast of Fife and is just south of St Andrews, not far from Carnoustie.

l. 12 *Pleiades:* a cluster of small stars in the constellation of Taurus. The group of flying birds shares some aspects of the appearance of a group of stars in the sky.

ll. 27–32 She imagines her sons in the future as students graduating at the end of their university course, serving as lieutenants in the Army or Navy, getting married, or becoming successful writers or politicians.

Mallaig Harbour Resembles Heaven in Spring Sunshine

Mallaig is one of the ports on the west coast of Scotland from which fishing boats sail out to the fishing grounds and car-ferries leave for the Island of Skye.

Poem to my Daughter

'' 1–14 Anne Stevenson plays with the different possible meanings of the words *have* and *deliver*, in the context of childbirth.

l. 11 *hostages to fortune:* Bacon, in his essay *Of Marriage and Single Life* says that 'He that hath wife and children, hath given hostages to fortune: for they are impediments to great enterprises, either of virtue or of mischief.'

If I Could Paint Essences

l. 5 *coltsfoot:* a common weed with a hairy stem and a yellow flower, like a small dandelion.

Green Mountain, Black Mountain

l. 23 *Terra Nova:* these Latin words mean *the new earth.*

l. 31 *mowin:* this is the dialect word used by the inhabitants of Vermont for a hayfield, i.e. a field where the grass is intended to be mown.

l. 60 Welsh legends say that King Arthur and his warriors are sleeping in a cave between the Black Mountains and Carmarthen. At the peal of a bell, says the legend, he will rise to rescue Wales when she is in grave danger.

l. 67 Teyrnon and Pryderi are characters in Welsh legends who are associated with horses.

l. 69 *Annwfn:* this is the underworld, the world of the dead, in Welsh legends. All the creatures who exist there have only two colours – red and white.

l. 97 *New Haven:* this town is comparatively near to Green Mountain. Both are in New England.

ll. 158–166 The quotations are from a book by William Bradford telling the story of the Pilgrim Fathers. They spent some time in Boston (Lincolnshire, England) and Leyden (Holland) before they sailed from Plymouth to New England.

l. 198 The *Razumovskis* are the string quartets which Beethoven composed and dedicated to a keen amateur violinist, the Russian nobleman, Prince Razumovsky.

ll. 199–201 At the time when her father was encouraging her to play music, Hitler was transporting Polish Jews to gas chambers and Russian and German armies were fighting in Vienna, as the Russians began their westward advance.

ll. 238–241 The four lines beginning '*I hate it*' are an attempt to imitate the song of a thrush.

Swifts

l. 5 The swift, which seems to carry out the motion of a scythe against the sky, moves like an arrow (a *bolt*) that creates a notch (or *nock*) in the archer's bow.